I0521111

ii

START ANYWHERE

Do Something So Something Happens

Circles of Change from Vergil's Coffee Table

by Chris Judson

First edition: 2026
Published by
Vergil's Coffee Table
Middlebury, Indiana
Cover and interior design by the author.
Printed in the United States of America.
ISBN: 979-8-9941399-0-5
Library of Congress Control Number: 2026900582

For Lori

Acknowledgments

"I am a part of all I have met"
— Alfred, Lord Tennyson, *"Ulysses"*

This book traveled a long road, and I didn't walk it alone.

To Lori — my partner in all things — thank you for your steady presence, your deep wisdom, and your willingness to walk with me through every gate, every turn, every return.

To Evan and Colin — who made me a father and continue to teach me what it means to pay attention.

To the friends and fellow readers who gave time, insight, and heart to early drafts — Erica, Jeff, Cindy, Jennifer, and Lori — thank you for helping me see more clearly what this book could become.

To the teachers, students, colleagues, and creative souls who have shared their stories over the years — this book is shaped by your courage and questions.

To Raina and Marissa and their staffs — who made the coffee corner table feel like home.

And to you, reader — thank you for picking up this book and stepping into these pages. May you find a rhythm that meets you where you are.

Prelude

Dear Friend,

Thank you for picking up this book and opening it. I'm glad you're here, even if you don't yet know why this book found its way into your hands.

My name is Chris Judson. For most of my life, I've lived in schools—first as a student, then as an English teacher. I'm the kind of teacher who avoids telling strangers on airplanes what I do, mostly because the conversation quickly turns to grammar apologies or memories of an English class that didn't quite land. What I've always been more interested in isn't correctness, but attention. I'm curious about what people care about, what they notice, and what they're trying to say. If you give me time, I'll ask enough questions until we land on the thing that matters to you.

That curiosity became my work. I spent twenty-four years in classrooms, helping reluctant students discover—sometimes accidentally—that they could read, write, and respond to the world. Later, I stepped out of the classroom and spent several more years supporting and coaching teachers, traveling across Indiana and beyond. And then, unexpectedly, that season ended.

What followed was a move to a tiny house in the Sonoran Desert near Tucson, Arizona. Two adults, a cat, and 233 square feet. A shift not just in where we lived, but in how we lived. Running had already been part of my life for years—marathons, especially, something I had returned to more than once over two decades. During this season, though, that practice took on a different weight: long, slow efforts that required patience, persistence, and attention to small increments of progress. Around this same stretch of years, I found myself walking through Torii gates in Japan—literal thresholds marking entry and attention, not arrival. Learning, the tiny house, and the marathon became lived metaphors, not ideas I set out to collect, but experiences I found myself inside.

Some would call that period of my life a transition. And in the obvious sense, it was. A career pause. A geographic move. A change in pace and structure. At times, it felt disorienting and uncertain enough that I jokingly referred to it as my own "valley of the shadow of death"—less dramatic in fact than in feeling. I wondered whether I had made a mistake walking away from work I loved. I hoped, quietly, that something would happen if I just started doing something.

That something turned out to be writing and reflection.

But what surprised me most wasn't the large arc of change—it was what I began to notice in between. I realized that transition isn't only something that happens during major life events like graduations, weddings, or funerals. It's happening all the time. In the moments between tasks. In the walk from one room to another. In the drive to the store. In the pause before beginning again.

When I slowed down enough to notice those in-between moments, they became teachers. Not loud ones—quiet ones. Moments that invited attention, presence, and return. Sometimes I jotted a note. Sometimes I recorded a voice memo. Sometimes I simply noticed and moved on. Over time, those small acts of attention reshaped how I understood change itself.

This book grew out of that practice.

You could read it straight through, cover to cover. But you don't have to. You might think of the reflections here as small disruptions—moments to pause, notice, and return—rather than steps in a sequence that must be completed.

One way to read this book is exactly as its title suggests: Start anywhere. Read a reflection that catches your eye. Sit with the prompt that follows. Wander. Skip around. Follow curiosity. For some readers, this freedom feels like relief—a release from the pressure to finish quickly or read correctly.

Another way to use this book is more deliberate and slow. You might choose to read one reflection a day, or one a week. Read, respond, pause. Let the ideas linger. Some readers pair this rhythm with the simple web-based practices that accompany each section, using them as reminders to notice their own transitions over time. Others prefer a notebook, a margin, or a quiet walk. All of these are enough.

You don't need to finish this book to use it well.

The apps mentioned throughout are not requirements. They exist as gentle prompts—ways to interrupt the trance of busyness and invite attention back to the present. If they help, use them. If not, leave them aside. The real work happens between the readings, in your own noticing.

More than anything, I want to offer permission: to begin, to pause, to return, and to begin again.

If it helps, you might imagine me not as a guide who leads, but as a companion who walks alongside—much like Vergil walking with Dante, attentive but not in charge. This is your path. I'm simply here for part of the walk.

Peace,
Chris
Tucson, AZ 06 Jan 2026

Table of Contents

Acknowledgments... viii

Prelude ix

Table of Contents... xii

Engage 1

ENGAGE: The Gates We Walk Through 3

A Funny Thing Happened on the Way to the Coffee Shop 7

Look Homeward, Saguaro 11

In Praise of Generative AI (ChatGPT and friends) 15

The Vestibule: In Praise of First Drafts 19

Gone with the Wind (and the Dust)..23

The Stranger in the Parking Lot...27

A Room with a View (of the Parking Lot) 30

Home Again. Home Again. 34

"Once More to the Cloud"...39

Engage Wrap (Torii Gates / The Vestibule)................................42

Reduce 45

REDUCE: The Bike Never Came 47

The Things We Carried (and the Ones We Left Behind)..............51

You Can't Take It With You (At Least for Now) 55

Of Cholla and Men...59

The Tiny House and the Fog...62

On the Road, Still...66

The Hunger Games (and the Leftovers) 69

Reduce Wrap (Tiny House / Turn) 72

Persist 75

PERSIST: Tom Made Me Do It..77

Zen and the Art of Water Heater Maintenance 81

The Warren and the Wide World: Writing Between Safety and Discovery.....85

When Things Fall Apart (and So Do We)....................................90

A Farewell to Ladders: Much Ado About Fastening....................93

The Play's the Thing (Even When You Lose the Queen) 97

All Quiet on the Desert Front..101

A Kind of Homegoing *104*

The Persistence of Steps *109*

"The Road Not Yet Paved" *113*

Persist Wrap (Marathon / Circles of Change) *117*

Practice Apps — Where Reflection Meets Action **119**

Practice Apps — Begin, Act, Reflect *121*

The Vestibule — A Place for Quiet Focus & Uninterrupted Writing *125*

Turn — A Record of Follow-Through *127*

Circles of Change — A Guided Journey from Vergil's Coffee Table *129*

The Practice of Returning *132*

Afterword — Create Your Own Metaphor *134*

If You'd Like to Sit With This a Little Longer *136*

Coffee Notes *139*

About the Author *143*

Colophon *145*

Vergil's Coffee Table *149*

Engage

The invitation to begin again —through fear, through joy, through the gates we walk anyway.

ENGAGE: The Gates We Walk Through

Engage — The Torii Gates

When Lori and I decided to travel to Japan, I told myself I would be ready. I downloaded Duolingo, committed to the daily lessons, and kept a streak for 169 days straight. I could identify hiragana, recite vocabulary, and earn digital badges like Mario stars. But most of the time, I wasn't learning—I was performing.

Fifteen minutes a day became ritual without depth. I could say words in my head, but not in my mouth. I had studied the language, but never spoken it.

When we arrived in Tokyo, that became clear fast. Menus blurred. Conversations moved too quickly. I smiled, bowed, pointed at pictures, and hoped for context clues. Lori tried phrases she had practiced, and people understood her. I tried the same words, and they floated away before they reached my tongue.

It wasn't the words that failed me—it was my lack of embodiment. Learning only counts when it's lived.

And then, we reached Kyoto.

The day was damp, the sky misted with light rain. We climbed the mountain path at Fushimi Inari, where thousands of orange Torii gates stand shoulder to shoulder, a long tunnel of light and repetition. Each gate bears inscriptions—blessings, prayers, the names of donors. Each one marks a crossing from the ordinary to the sacred.

As I walked beneath them, I thought of all my small attempts at mastery—the languages, the plans, the projects that lived mostly in my head. The gates reminded me: this isn't about mastery. It's about motion. You don't earn the passage; you step through it.

Engagement, like those gates, is not a single door you open once. It's a practice of showing up again and again.

That's the invitation of The Vestibule: to begin. Not to perfect, not to perform. Just to begin.

Fifteen minutes. One gate at a time.

Write the line that comes. Then another. Don't polish. Don't backtrack. Move through.

Each word becomes a threshold. Each sentence, a gate.

The desert where we now live reminds me of those gates, too. The saguaros rise like orange posts against the sky—solemn, repetitive, marking another kind of sacred path. Between Japan's rain and Arizona's dust, I've learned that engagement is not about pace or polish. It's about presence.

You start where you are. You say what you can. You show up for the act, not the applause.

Because learning—like writing, like living—doesn't happen by thinking about it.

It happens by walking through the gate.

A Funny Thing Happened on the Way to the Coffee Shop

Not Retired, a Snowbird, or Noisy (I Think)

It started with a label. Or rather, three.

We've been in Tucson long enough now that I've been called a few things: noisy, retired, and a snowbird. None of them quite sit right. But like most labels, they reveal more than they hide — especially when you start asking what's underneath.

Label One: Noisy

Most mornings, I work from my usual seat at the Starbucks near Picture Rocks. If you know the layout, I'm near the counter with the oat milk, the recycling bins, and the small table that catches just enough light to see Sombrero Hill out the window. It's the unofficial corner office for my remote consulting life.

One Wednesday, I was mid-Zoom with a friend from Alabama when an older man — who sits with his wife at the same spot each week — leaned over from two tables away and said flatly, "You're noisy."

I paused. Took out an earbud. Looked around. Everyone else was talking, too.

"You need to move," he said again.

I didn't argue. I moved my setup to the patio and finished

the call outside. When he left, I tried to make eye contact, but he looked past me. Even now, months later, he avoids my gaze. He wears T-shirts from Hawaii. I think he's ex-military—maybe Navy. A Yankee's tattoo on his calf. He has a story I don't know. Maybe I'm part of a story he tells about that guy who Zoomed at Starbucks.

It stung. Not just the interruption, but the certainty. You are noisy. No space for conversation, no middle ground.

And yet—I can be noisy. In high school, my friend Russ and I almost got kicked out of Round Table Pizza in Santa Rosa for being too loud, too animated, too much. We were just trying to amuse ourselves, maybe impress some girls. That memory lingers, too.

So maybe it's not about volume. Maybe it's about visibility.

Label Two: Retired

Back in Boston, at a national conference, my friend from Alabama (the same one from the Zoom call) organized a surprise retirement party. I opened a card that said, "You're retired now!"—complete with a wine joke.

I laughed, sort of. But also: I'm not retired.

Or am I?

I no longer get a direct deposit every two weeks. After decades of a paycheck showing up—without needing to cash it or touch it—that rhythm stopped. And with it, a certain identity I hadn't realized I carried. Teacher. Director. Salaried professional.

Now I work on my own terms. But does that make me retired? Or just rewired?

I remember talking to a friend from Colorado: Am I retired? Or just reframing what I do?

The answer, still, is: I don't know.

Label Three: Snowbird

Snowbird season in Tucson is real. It shapes traffic patterns and dinner wait times. It fills RV parks and golf courses. And it carries its own subtle judgment. Oh, the snowbirds are back.

Earlier this year, we were newcomers. So when someone asked if we were snowbirds, I said yes—easiest shorthand.

But a friend, someone I knew from my 2009 "40 Plays in 40 Days" project in Virginia—now an artistic director—challenged that. "You're not snowbirds," he said. "You're Firebirds. You stayed past March."

He was right. Most left by early March. We stayed through the triple digits, into May. We weren't just escaping winter. We were living here.

Still, it's a strange thing—to be grouped, named, and sorted into seasonal categories. Firebird felt better. It made space for our version of the story.

And What Else? Tell Me More

The desert has its own kind of clarity. It strips things back. Out here, we're surrounded by saguaros blooming on their own strange schedules, by cholla that glow and sting, by neighbors building sheds and planning for the future. It reminds me how little we control—and how much we long to belong.

I've been called noisy. I've been labeled retired. I've been sorted as a snowbird. And each of those says something—but never the whole thing.

Maybe what I really want—what we all want—is the follow-up question. Not just what are you? But:

And What else? Tell me more.

Because the real work isn't in the labeling. It's in the listening. And that's where the stories begin.

Your Turn:

What's a label someone's given you lately—and what's the part of your story they didn't see?

Write a quick scene, memory, or moment that reveals the fuller truth.

Look Homeward, Saguaro

What does it mean to belong—to a place, to a rhythm, to a story that doesn't begin and end with people?

When someone recently asked, "Who's your community out there in Arizona?" I paused.

Not because I didn't have an answer, but because I didn't have a neat one. I didn't say a church group, or workplace, or friend circle. I said Ken and Barbie (yes, their real names). I said Craig across the way, and Steve 1, Steve 2, Steve 3. Theresa with her afternoon walks, sometimes accompanied by Nik. A few others. Enough to make the place feel known, if not always understood.

This is Picture Rocks—not quite a town, more like a scattered brushstroke of desert dwellings, a rhythm of comings and goings, a place where Google Maps shrugs and neighbors wave.

It isn't always pretty. But it's real. And maybe that's the better kind of beautiful.

Community with a Spine

We didn't just inherit human neighbors—we inherited saguaros. Some more than a century old, rooted deep and reaching tall. I might have named one Kevin—he bloomed early, generously, from his east-facing arm. I read that early bloomers sacrifice more: they offer pollen to the first round of pollinators—bats, bees, birds—without any promise of return.

And that stuck with me.

Because that's what community does, too. It gives first. It reaches out.

Sometimes, things bloom. Sometimes, they don't.

The saguaros don't complain. They just adjust.

Neighbors Without Names

I used to think community was only human. But the longer we stay, the more I see otherwise.

The palo verdes humming with bees.

The cholla we curse and clear, but which shelters the pack rats.

The mourning doves perched like punctuation on a fence post.

The coyotes who remind us we are not the only ones awake.

They're part of the rhythm now. They show up, too.

I've been reading *A Literary Field Guide to the Sonoran Desert* and *The Saguaro Cactus: A Natural History*, and in both, the landscape is treated not as scenery, but as voice. Not as backdrop, but as character.

And that's what I've come to believe: not all neighbors speak.

But all of them say something, if we're listening.

What We Try, What Fails, What Still Belongs

Not every conversation becomes a friendship. Not every bloom becomes fruit. Some things fall, wither, fade. There are beetles on the ground. Blooms that never caught the wind.

Still, it mattered that they tried.

Community, like the desert, doesn't guarantee outcome. It asks presence. It rewards attention. And it humbles you with its silences.

Sometimes, connection doesn't wave back. But you show up anyway. You water the thing. You watch. You name. You notice.

The Practice of Staying

Colin, our youngest, joined us for a few days in the spring. He listened quietly as we told him which cactus had bloomed, which had died, the old man who sold honey out of his pickup. At some point, he might have smiled and said something like, "You two are really into this, huh?"

Yes. We are.

Because this is how we stay.

Even if we're only here for a season, even if it's just part of the year—we're not just passing through. We're learning. We're tending. We're showing up for the ordinary.

And maybe that's enough.

Maybe that's what it means to belong.

Your Turn:

Who's in your landscape?

Make a list of the neighbors you usually overlook—human or otherwise. Write one line about what they offer to your sense of place.

In Praise of Generative AI (ChatGPT and friends)

Neither a Silver Bullet Nor a Werewolf (or both)

My first car was technically a 1968 Chevy Biscayne, with that "three on the tree" for its manual column shifter. It had multiple shades of green and silver, steered like a boat, and was as far from sleek as you can imagine. After college, though, I bought my first brand-new car: a 1988 Ford Festiva L. The "L," I found out, meant "limited"— "God's" air conditioning, four on the floor, and an AM/FM radio, to be precise. I decked it out with Sparkomatic speakers and a Radio Shack tape deck that didn't quite fit but worked anyway. It was perfect for delivering checks by day and pizzas by night during that Napa Valley summer of 1988.

Over the years, there were other cars: a memorable 1993 Ford Escort wagon with a perpetually failing muffler that announced my arrival from five blocks away. Now, in my later years, I've finally bought the vehicle I've been eyeing for two years: a white Ford Maverick Hybrid. It's practical, efficient, and—being a hybrid—perhaps a bit of an ethical or political statement.

Since I started driving it, I've noticed every white truck on the road. Specifically, I high-five other white Mavericks through my window. It's fascinating how once you're tuned into something new, you start seeing it everywhere. This kind of attentional bias (perhaps frequency illusion bias) applies to many areas of life, including education and technology.

Seeing What's New Everywhere

Generative AI, much like my white Maverick, is everywhere. It's dominating conversations in education, particularly in English classrooms. We've been here before, though. In the early days of the internet, Wikipedia, and even Google, educators expressed similar fears. Back then, we worried students would merely copy text from these newfangled tools rather than think critically or creatively.

But those tools didn't end writing or creativity. Instead, they changed how we approached teaching. The same can happen with AI if we let it. As Susan Barber aptly said during a 2023 NCTE panel on Generative AI, and I'm paraphrasing: "Don't panic. Be curious."

Generative AI, such as ChatGPT, offers opportunities to rethink how we use time in our classrooms. It's not a replacement for teaching—just as a car doesn't replace walking, but can make some journeys more efficient. It's a reminder to reflect on our practice, asking what we truly aim for in composition instruction.

What We Can Control

Here's the thing: we might fear that generative AI will replace creativity, but sometimes, our assignments don't encourage creativity in the first place. Instead of focusing on what AI might do, let's refocus on what we can do.

Take a moment to pause and consider this activity:

1. Write down what's on your mind about generative AI.

2. Then, write some more.

3. Breathe.

4. Circle/underline/annotate 3-7 interesting ideas or sentences from your freewrite.

5. Draw a large circle ("Concerns") and then draw a smaller circle ("Control") inside that large circle.

6. Transfer your 3-7 ideas into two circles: one for things within your control and one for things outside it.

Such an exercise can help clarify what matters most and what's worth our energy.

For example, in classrooms, the most significant area of influence we have is time. If the heart of composition instruction is to get students to write more, we need to spend more time practicing writing in class—not just assigning it as homework. Think about the "why" students love sports or the arts and the "how" they get there: most of their time is spent practicing, with occasional performances. Writing should be the same.

Generative AI: Friend or Foe?

Generative AI tools like ChatGPT aren't perfect. Like humans, they fumble on first drafts and miss the mark occasionally. But they can also handle repetitive tasks and free up time for deeper work. Think of them as the modern equivalent of MapQuest or Yelp or Alta Vista: mostly helpful, with the occasional misstep.

By embracing AI thoughtfully, we can use it to enhance productivity, explore new creative avenues, and deepen our understanding of writing and learning. It's not a silver bullet or a werewolf; it's just another tool in the toolbox.

Back to the Road

The Maverick has more room in the bed than one thinks-- even enough to bring all one needs to Arizona.

Today, after yesterday's wind and dust, I'll admit my white Maverick needs a wash—it's no longer gleaming in the sun. But I'll keep noticing white trucks and waving at fellow Maverick drivers. Just like noticing the familiar in the new, generative AI reminds us to see the possibilities while staying rooted in what we know works: practice, curiosity, and the willingness to learn.

Your Turn:

What's one small, surprising thing already in your life—your version of the white Maverick—that's inviting you to pay closer attention?

Take a moment to name it, then jot down what it might be trying to teach you.

The Vestibule: In Praise of First Drafts

The room before the room where things happen

Earlier in March, as we prepared to leave the desert rhythms of Casa Saguaro for a stretch back in Indiana, it hit me again how much space matters—not just physical space, but mental space too.

Before we left, I started building something. Quietly. Almost accidentally.

The Vestibule.

It's not a program. Not a course. It's a space. A place to step inside and write.

But here's the catch: it's a space that honors the first draft—not the polished product, not the curated version you post on LinkedIn, but the real, rough, uncertain first attempt.

Why a Vestibule?

A vestibule isn't the main room. It's the small, transitional space between the outside world and whatever happens next.

That's how I see writing. Good writing—real writing—doesn't happen in grand, final flourishes. It happens when we step inside, close the door behind us, and give ourselves permission to stay in the messy middle.

But The Vestibule is more than just a small room.

It's a reference point—a nod to Dante's *Inferno*, where souls trapped in the Vestibule linger in eternal hesitation, unwilling to commit to either good or evil.

They wander, circling forever, stuck between intention and action.

Writers know that space too.

It's the blank page. The stalled draft. The endless distractions that keep us moving but never advancing.

The Vestibule isn't meant to trap you there.

It's meant to move you through it—beyond hesitation, beyond limbo.

First Drafts Matter

Here's what I believe:

- First drafts aren't failures. They're the beginning of momentum.

- First drafts aren't meant to impress. They're meant to reveal.

- First drafts aren't ugly. They're alive.

When we rush past the first draft stage, we lose the only part of the process that's truly ours—the unfiltered thinking, the wild idea, the mistake that turns into a breakthrough.

The Vestibule gives permission to slow down and stay there.

To not judge.

To not compare.

To write without constantly asking, Is this good enough yet?

Because it's not about being good enough.

It's about moving forward.

Building the Practice

In practice, The Vestibule looks like:
A predictable rhythm of showing up (even when it's messy)
A small space to land, think, draft, and breathe
No immediate audience, no external pressure
Just the act of returning, again and again, to the work
And just like Dante needed Vergil to guide him through the Inferno, sometimes we need a system, a steady hand, to guide us forward—especially when the temptation to stall is strong.

It's not about creating masterpieces.

It's about becoming someone who writes instead of someone who talks about writing.

A Final Thought: The Door Is Open

In some ways, Casa Saguaro was a vestibule—a space between one part of life and the next. So is The Estate in Indiana. So are the early mornings at Starbucks when I open the laptop and just start typing without knowing where it's going.

We need more vestibules.

More spaces that honor the start of things, not just the finish.

So this is your invitation:

Come inside. Bring your first draft. Keep moving. The only way out is through.

Your Turn:

What wants to begin?
Open a blank page. Write without stopping for 15 minutes. Don't aim for brilliance—just motion. One line at a time.

Gone with the Wind (and the Dust)

The Weather Just Is

It was another windy day in Picture Rocks. The kind where it feels like Zeus himself is reminding us that "playtime is canceled." No walk. No bike ride. No run.

At some point, you learn to stop arguing with the wind.

I used to think I could will the day into being what I wanted — schedule it, plan it, optimize it. Now I understand that some days don't bend to your preferences. They bend you instead.

The Extremes We Live In

Here in the Sonoran Desert, we've been learning to live with extremes. One day it's 49°F, the next, 101°F. The wind howls. The sun bakes. The night cools just enough to let you believe you'll sleep.

We're still working on what we call "climate control" — trying to normalize the inside of our tiny house against the chaos of the outside. And sometimes it feels more like we're managing emotions than temperature.

It's taught us something about acceptance. The desert doesn't ask for your approval. It doesn't care how you feel about the forecast.

The Weather in South Carolina

Last week, we were in Columbia, South Carolina, for my nephew and sister-in-law's college graduation. Back in the land of humidity — mosquitoes, damp shirts, and air you can wear.

Walking back from dinner at an Asian restaurant, I found myself complaining. Not just noting the heat. Complaining. That kind of running commentary that starts with "this is awful" and spirals into "why is it like this?" as if my preferences matter to the climate.

I vented to Lori. She listened patiently. But really, what was I hoping would change?

Later I remembered an essay by William F. Buckley called "Why Don't We Complain?" In it, Buckley describes the strange tendency we have to remain silent about things we could change, and then erupt about things we can't. The air is too hot on the train, but we won't ask the attendant. The movie projector is out of focus, but no one stands up to speak. Meanwhile, we stew.

And sometimes, we do speak — but for what?

Circles of Influence, Revised

The old model still helps: Circle of Influence vs. Circle of Concern. But I've been wondering if there's another metaphor — maybe something more desert-native. Something like a cactus.

A cactus doesn't try to shade the whole desert. It roots deeply, stores what it can, adapts. Some seasons it blooms; others, it survives.

What if instead of trying to "control" the weather — or the day, or the outcomes — we just learned to notice what we can adapt to? What shade we can make. What routines keep us sane. What tea or coffee to drink when the wind starts up again.

Because sometimes, the best we can do isn't control — it's response.

What Complaints Reveal

When I complain about the weather, I'm not really talking about the weather. I'm naming a mismatch between expectation and reality.

The weather just is.

But I am not always okay with that. I want things to feel fair. Comfortable. Predictable. And when they aren't, I reach for commentary. I reach for certainty. And sometimes, I reach for blame.

But weather doesn't take feedback.

A Better Forecast

What I'm learning (slowly, stubbornly) is this: most of my life is not shaped by external conditions. It's shaped by how I receive them. Whether I fixate or let go. Whether I whine or adapt. Whether I brace or breathe.

And so, I'm trying something different.

When the weather doesn't cooperate, I put on a kettle of hot water.

When the forecast disappoints, I reframe the plan.

When the wind says "not today," I try to hear "not yet."

Because maybe the real forecast isn't about temperature or pressure.

Maybe it's just this:

"Today, there will be weather. How will you show up?"

Your Turn:

What can you shade, not control?

List three things that frustrate you right now. Then circle the one you can respond to—not fix, not fight, just respond with presence.

The Stranger in the Parking Lot

The small distance between judgment and empathy

It started with a bottle of spearmint oil.

Early in our Arizona stay, we came across a local market — just a weekend pop-up in a Barnes & Noble parking lot off Ina Road. One of the booths sold essential oils, hand-bottled, and I thought: why not use this instead of a commercial air freshener? I had read somewhere — probably a college study with limited scope — that peppermint oil could help with alertness. So I bought a little wood diffuser for the truck and dabbed it with peppermint. It worked — or at least felt like it did.

When I ran low, I figured I'd try spearmint instead.

This morning, after working on a project at the library, I walked to the truck and caught the new scent — spearmint, warmed by the Arizona sun. And it hit me: spearmint really does just smell like chewing gum. Not sure I like that.

But something else happened on that walk.

I passed a woman — maybe in her 30s — walking with a cane, clearly favoring her right hip or leg. And without warning, my first internal response was: Well, at least that's not me.

The thought surprised me. It startled me. Because it wasn't just a reflex. It was a judgment — an unspoken ranking of her life versus mine. It came with all kinds of assumptions: about wholeness, about health, about how we unconsciously compare ourselves to others as a way to measure... what? Gratitude?

Worth?

It reminded me of something I once heard from Brené Brown — the difference between empathy and sympathy. I used to show that animated video in workshops, the one with her voiceover explaining how unhelpful it can be to say "at least..." when someone's in a dark place. "At least you can still..." "At least it's not worse..." We think we're helping. But really, we're creating distance. We're reinforcing the gap between us and them.

And today I caught myself doing just that — with a stranger.

Comparison breeds judgment. Not just of others, but of ourselves. That impulse to say at least I'm not... doesn't lift anyone up — it reinforces the idea that someone else's pain is useful only as a contrast to our own comfort.

So what's the alternative?

Maybe it's presence. Maybe it's sitting — with the discomfort, with the judgment, with the awkwardness of not knowing what to say. Mindfulness teaches that when a thought arises, you don't push it away. You notice it. You let it be there. If you try to swat it down, it just comes back — like Neko the cat pawing at your leg.

Instead, you sit.

You say: I don't know what to say, but I'm glad you told me.

You say it to others. You say it to yourself.

And in this case, you say it to the version of you who reacted with distance instead of closeness.

As I kept walking, the woman with the cane moved on — faster than I expected. She's out of sight now. But maybe she was there just long enough for the thought to sit with me. Just long enough to remind me how easy it is to drift into judgment — and how hard, and necessary, it is to return to empathy.

Oh, and for the record: spearmint still smells like gum. I think I'll go back to peppermint.

Your Turn:

Catch the reflex. Stay with it.

Recall a moment when you compared yourself to someone else. What did that reflex reveal—and what might empathy say instead?

A Room with a View (of the Parking Lot)

When a quiet moment in Starbucks becomes a reminder of what we carry

It was a typical afternoon at the Starbucks near Casa Saguaro (the tiny house) in Picture Rocks. I'd settled into a corner table, intent on catching up on writing, near the wide window that overlooks the parking lot. It's a modest view: a row of sun-bleached cars in the Safeway parking lot, the occasional breeze shifting a paper napkin across the asphalt. But still, it's a favorite spot. You can see Safford Peak (Sombrero Peak to the locals) in the foreground and Panther Peak off to the right. You can drink coffee from a ceramic mug. You can breathe.

A woman walked in with her son. She gave him a soft instruction — "go ahead and sit by the windows" — and went off to place their order. Without hesitation, he took the seat directly across from me. I don't think he noticed me at first. He just started watching the cars pass by. His arms rose and fell in wide arcs, mimicking their motion, his eyes full of wonder. He was, I'd guess, around ten. And in those first few moments, it felt like he and I were in two separate worlds, only incidentally sharing a table.

At one point, he glanced in my direction. I smiled and said, "I like sitting here too."

We didn't speak after that, but we sat together. I turned back to my screen, but only partly. I was aware of his presence — not as an interruption, but as a kind of gift. These are the things that shape a day sometimes: the unexpected company of someone delighting in the moment, unfiltered.

Driving home through Saguaro National Forest that afternoon, I found myself tracing a memory I hadn't visited in a while. A quiet thread that had started unraveling years ago — my first panic attack.

It gave me pause. Lately, my mind had been full. Tight-chested. A particular flavor of anxiety — quiet but persistent. Not a panic, but a pressure. The kind that says: You should be further along than this.

It brought me back to a long history I don't often talk about.

There was a time, after my mother died, when I couldn't sleep. That kind of buzzing, high-alert feeling. A first adult panic attack. I remember walking Third Street with Lori in the middle of the night, trying to calm down. A sense that my body had turned on me — tight chest, racing thoughts, no clear trigger. Trying every strategy — sleep aids, new diets, stricter routines — hoping for a fix.

But as I traced it back further, I realized I'd known that feeling much longer. Back to a weekend trip to Madison, when I had to pull over on the Skyway and figure out how to drive through a panic. Back to a college job where a chest flutter sent me to a cardiologist. Back to asthma attacks as a child — waiting for my mom to return with an adrenaline shot, hoping that relief would come soon

And further still, back to early childhood. Foster care. A crib that moved across the room because I rocked it, alone.

The anxiety wasn't new. What was new — what is new — is the naming of it. The refusal to push it away. The learning, over time, that even these feelings are part of the pattern. That what begins with tightness can end in breath, and maybe rest.

All that surfaced again, quietly, as I drove through those

winding desert roads. Sometimes healing feels like that—an echo that comes back not with panic, but with gentleness. With the sense that, maybe, I'm still learning how to sit beside that child in me. The one who once rocked his crib across the room, trying to self-soothe. The one who needed someone nearby to say, "It's okay. I like being here too."

Back at Starbucks, the boy's mother returned. She glanced around and noticed where her son had settled—still watching the traffic, still beside me. She approached our table with a soft smile and said, "Thank you for being so kind. He just likes to watch the cars."

Then she added:

"I've given up on apologizing. I used to say sorry all the time, but I can't control this. So now I just say thank you."

I told her there was no need to thank me—that I liked sitting there too. But I haven't forgotten her words.

Not sorry.

Thank you.

There's a quiet power in that shift. A posture of presence. Of grace. And maybe even the beginning of something that looks like peace.

Your Turn:

What's sitting beside you today?

Think of a small moment that interrupted your routine. What did it remind you of—and what part of you needed that reminder?

Home Again. Home Again.

Out, back, again—learning to return with presence

We crossed the state line on a soft day in May. Not quite cold, but definitely not desert. The traffic started somewhere outside Indiana, and by the time we pulled into the driveway, everything was bright and loud. Too green, I kept thinking. Too close. The trees were all shouting in chlorophyll.

Cletus had mowed the yard for us again—didn't know when we were coming back but did it anyway. That's the kind of neighbor he is. Quiet. Present. Not fuzzy, not sitcom kind—just steady. Like the ones back in Picture Rocks. You don't ask for help, but it's there anyway.

We unpacked. Neko the cat immediately found his old spot near the south-facing window and started sleeping more on our laps. I think he likes this house. Maybe we all do—eventually. But that first week, the house smelled like closed windows, and the carpet was too soft. Everything inside was humid. Even silence here hums with cicadas and the low thrum of RV transport and Amish buggy traffic.

The transition was harder than expected. I kept thinking I should be able to slip right back into Midwest rhythm. I've done this before. But this time, I felt clipped. Trimmed back—like that too-short haircut I got the week we returned. The one that undid all the Arizona wildness Lori said she liked. There's a metaphor there I haven't quite unpacked.

People asked how I was doing. I said "fine." But the truth is, I wanted to complain. About the weather. About the noise. About how fast it all felt.

And I couldn't. Not really. I'd already written about that.

...

A few days after we got back, I saw one of the local school buses making its slow turn onto our road—the same yellow curve, the same hiss of brakes. It made me think of a book we used to read to Evan and Colin when they were small: *School Bus* by Donald Crews. It's spare and rhythmic, like so many of his books. Not much happens, but everything moves—buses go this way and that, full and empty, crossing the town. At the end of the day, they come back. Home again. Home again.

I remember how we loved the simplicity of that cadence—not just the rhythm of the students, but the rhythm of those who do the transporting. It's all motion with purpose. And when I saw that bus again, years later and hundreds of miles from where we first read the book aloud, I felt something click. That line had stayed with me.

The rhythm of going out, and coming back.

The rhythm of return.

...

A few days later, I set up shop at the Starbucks near the bypass. My usual spot was open—small table, partial view of the parking lot, enough light to squint at the screen without full glare. I was mid-email when the Wi-Fi hiccupped, just long enough for the man behind me to mutter, "Oh come on," like the universe owed him speed.

I almost laughed—until I realized I'd refreshed my inbox six times in the past hour. That desert patience I'd earned? Already leaking.

...

My body has been talking to me, too.

The sudden swing from dry to damp triggers my breathing. Asthma again—like third grade, running in from recess unable to catch a breath. It's not always the allergens. Sometimes it's just the shift. Or the emotions. Sometimes I feel it in my stomach first, like something turning over before I even know what the feeling is. IBS makes a great storyteller: exaggerated, blunt, unignorable.

I've learned not to fight it. To take a breath. Count to ten. Listen to what my body is trying to say before I decide what I think.

Sometimes the weather inside the house isn't the real problem. It's the one I bring in.

...

So here I am again. Back in Indiana. Writing. Watching the yard grow a little wilder each day. Letting the neighborhood reintroduce itself. Trying not to rush the rhythm.

The green still startles me. The rain still irritates me. Where's my blue, warm skies? But I'm learning to let it speak before I silence it with judgment.

And maybe that's all return really is: not a reset, but a reckoning. A walk through a familiar circle, slower this time.

We've done this before, of course—the great return. Packing up the slow life and dropping back into noise. But this time feels different. Maybe because the desert burned a slower rhythm into my bones. Or maybe because I'm finally learning that return is its own kind of practice.

A kind of engagement.

A kind of writing.

A kind of route you learn by heart.

Home is a mirror. It shows what you've learned—and what you've left behind.

Not every threshold is as obviously sacred as the Torii gates in Kyoto. Some are just familiar doorframes. A driveway. A morning routine. A yellow bus rounding the corner. And yet, there's something sacred in that rhythm too.

Because here's what I know now: you can't really "go back." You can only keep returning, each time a little more awake.

To keep noticing.
To stay present.
To make the ride home count.

...

Your Turn:

"What did you notice first when you returned?"

Write five sensory details—color, sound, texture, temperature, rhythm.

Then ask: Which ones still surprise you?

"Once More to the Cloud"

Just a drive, just some rain, and killing Lori's joy

When we got back to Indiana, the weather turned gray.

That first Saturday, it was almost warm, the air soft and full of promise — and then came the rain. By Sunday, the sky had gone flat, the kind of overcast that makes time feel heavy. I'd just posted a reflection about weather and mood, about how sunlight helps me see the world more clearly. It turns out that's easier to write from the desert, under a sky that opens every morning like a stage curtain.

Now I was back among clouds, the damp kind that dulls the edges of everything.

Lori didn't seem to mind.

We were driving down County Road 35, the road she takes from Middlebury to Goshen, a familiar route lined with Amish farms and quiet fields. She was so happy to see green again — the barns, the fences, the small shapes of spring animals in motion. Each time she spotted one, she said hello:

"Hi, baby cows."

"Hello, little lambs."

And she meant it.

She really did.

But I wasn't there for it.

I was sitting next to her, irritated, sullen, carrying a cloud big enough for two. Every "hi" made me flinch. At one point, I'm sure I wished the baby animals would just go away — which is not a sentence I'm proud of.

My mood began to spill. And before long, I could see it in her — the way her shoulders settled, the way her voice quieted. The joy I'd drained from the air was unmistakable. I'd changed the weather inside the car.

It's humbling when you realize, in real time, that you're the one changing the weather.

I've seen it happen before—at work, at home, even on long drives like this one. There's a moment when my mind locks onto judgment: this day is bad, this sky is wrong, this feeling should not be here. And then the judgment spreads faster than the thing itself.

The truth is, the gray wasn't the problem.

I was.

...

What makes it even more absurd is that I knew better.

Back at Casa Saguaro, in the desert, I'd lived through one of those rare, golden stretches that people later call their halcyon days. Everything felt alive—the light, the work, the daily rhythm. I'd drive past Twin Peaks each morning, the mountains edged in sunrise, hot air balloons rising over the ridgeline like punctuation marks in a sentence the sky was still writing.

Even then, I told myself: Remember this.

I knew those moments wouldn't last forever. They never do. But the awareness was its own kind of gratitude. Every day in that season, I could feel that I was awake to my own life.

And still, somewhere between that desert clarity and this gray Indiana sky, I forgot.

Maybe that's what nostalgia really is — not longing for a place, but for the version of yourself who was fully present when you were there.

...

The older I get, the more I realize joy isn't an event—it's a practice.

It's not something that happens to us; it's something we allow.

I came across a line recently:

"Do you want to know what my secret is? I don't mind what happens"

At first, it sounded flippant.

But the more I sit with it, the more I see its wisdom — a kind of spiritual detachment, not apathy.

It's about loosening the mind's grip on judgment.

Good day. Bad day.

Blue sky. Gray sky.

Nothing's changed but the story we tell about it.

...

That thought came back to me at the pharmacy the other day. They couldn't find Lori's prescription. The old me would've sighed, stewed, stared at the ceiling tiles. Instead, I took a breath. The pharmacist was doing her job. I didn't need to make it rain.

Presence, it turns out, is its own weather system.

...

Even now, as I write this, the sky outside is pale and undecided. Lori's in the kitchen, humming, the morning moving gently around her. Somewhere down the road, a field of calves and lambs are being greeted.

This time, I can join her.

I can let the sun back in.

...

Your Turn:

When has your weather changed someone else's day? What would it look like When did your internal "weather" —good or stormy —affect someone else's day?

Write about a time you noticed (or missed) that shift, and how you might make space for light next time.

Engage Wrap (Torii Gates / The Vestibule)

You've practiced showing up.

Sometimes awkwardly. Sometimes with more attention than before.

But you crossed the threshold.

Maybe now you notice how you begin.

Maybe you see what calls you forward.

What surprised you when you stepped in?

What line stayed with you after you stopped writing?

The gates are still there.

You can walk through one again anytime.

The first step is still here.

Reduce

The practice of letting go, of loosening our grip, of choosing space over clutter — internally and externally.

REDUCE: The Bike Never Came

Reduce — The Tiny House

On letting go of the wait, and learning to live in the meantime

The first days at Casa Saguaro were marked by one long, lingering expectation: things would happen quickly.

It's easy to believe that when you arrive with a list, momentum, and a portable Wi-Fi hotspot. The land—our acre in Picture Rocks—waited patiently. But we didn't. Within hours, we had internet installed. It was the fastest we'd ever had, and for a moment, we mistook that ease for pace.

Then came the post office.

We needed a mailing address. What we got was a window, a shrug, and a "someone will call you." They didn't. We returned. Again. And again. A supervisor finally promised results through a friend in Indianapolis. It came, eventually—just not when we expected it.

...

We spent those first weeks waiting on people who had promised things. And somewhere in the waiting, I started watching myself—how easily I default to refresh mode. Check again. Open the inbox. Reopen the app. See if the thing has come.

And it's not new.

When I was a kid, my father once told me he'd sent me a bike for Christmas. A big one. "It should've arrived already," he said. "It was shipped with the chocolate-brown truck."

UPS.

For weeks, I ran to the garage every time I heard a truck. I watched through the peephole. I imagined it. Maybe today. It never came.

I've spent years repeating that moment in different forms.

Refresh inbox.

Click "track package."

Open social media just to see if anything changed.

. . .

And I've started to wonder: What's the cost of that kind of attention?

Because while I'm fixated on what hasn't arrived, I'm often blind to what has.

This morning, it might be the barista remembering my name.

Yesterday, it was Lori waving through the window as I pulled up.

The day before, it was a text from a friend just checking in.

All of those things did arrive.

But they weren't on my list.

. . .

So now, I'm learning to reduce.

Not by removing things from my life, but by releasing my grip on how and when they show up.

I've even built myself a simple app: Turn.

It reminds me of the things I've said I'll do—for others, for myself—and nudges me to follow through. Not out of pressure, but out of presence.

It's my turn.

Not their promise.

. . .

We think we're waiting on the world.

Often, the world is waiting on us.

To show up.

To notice.

To let go of the bike that never came and open our eyes to the moment that did.

The Things We Carried (and the Ones We Left Behind)

Learning to carry only what carries us

We're back in Indiana for a week, stepping into the familiar space of The Estate, our 800-square-foot home, after weeks of living in Casa Saguaro, our 233-square-foot desert retreat.

The first thing I noticed? Too much space.

Walking through the house felt excessive — 60 feet from the kitchen to the bedroom instead of the 10 steps I'd grown used to. And the clothes? An entire spare room full, making me wonder: How did I ever think I needed all of this?

Defining Enough: The No-Trailer Rule

Not more than 13 weeks ago, we made a decision: only what fit in the bed of the Ford Maverick would come with us to Arizona. No trailer, no extra storage, no "just in case" packing.

At first, Lori and I wavered. Could we really fit everything essential into such a small space? The idea seemed abstract until we started measuring — taping out dimensions inside the house, stacking empty boxes in the garage, trying to see what "enough" actually looked like.

And then, it clicked.

We sorted by function: one box for clothes, one for kitchen essentials, one for work supplies. When I first started packing, I tossed in too much—things I thought I'd need, things I thought might be useful. But as I tried to fit everything into the defined space, I started removing, refining. Did I really need all these extra things? Would I actually use them? Bit by bit, I cut down until everything fit with room to spare.

I have to admit, though, the decision not to bring a trailer was met with some resistance—not just from Lori but from well-meaning friends and family who questioned whether we'd have everything we needed. And honestly, I questioned myself at times, too. There's something about space that invites us to fill it. But what if we resist that instinct? What if having less actually makes us more adaptable, more focused, and more in tune with what truly matters?

The Packing Puzzle: Finding Clarity Through Constraints

Even after measuring, we struggled to visualize how much would fit in the Maverick's bed. So, we took it a step further—bringing empty boxes into the house and assigning them by category. Clothes. Kitchen essentials. Work materials. Bathroom items. We treated the truck bed like a puzzle, stacking and shifting boxes until we found an arrangement that worked.

That process—physically mapping out space—transformed our thinking. Suddenly, we weren't making decisions based on abstract limits. We could see the boundaries, and that made the choices easier.

In some ways, this mirrors decision-making in work and life. When we don't define our limits, everything feels like a necessity. But when we establish clear boundaries—whether in projects, time, or commitments—we start seeing what's actually important.

Enough in Work and Life

This experience reminded me of how we approach our jobs, commitments, and daily routines. Just like packing for a small space, being intentional about our work—choosing what truly matters and cutting the rest—can be freeing.

Too often, we overfill our schedules the way we overfill our suitcases, out of fear—fear of not doing enough, not being enough, of missing out on something important. But real clarity comes from distilling our focus, not spreading ourselves too thin.

I've seen this happen in education, too. Teachers (myself included) often believe that more is better: more assignments, more policies, more strategies. But too much clutter suffocates clarity. Just like in our truck bed, every commitment should have a function. If it doesn't serve a purpose, it doesn't belong.

And yet, making those choices isn't always easy. There's a strange comfort in keeping "just in case" projects on our desks or holding onto obligations that no longer serve us. But at what cost? How often do we trade focus and energy for a sense of false security?

A Lesson from an Overstuffed Cab

One thing we didn't think through? Our overnight stop in Oklahoma City. We had packed our truck bed with precision, but when it came to what we needed for one night, we scrambled. Too many things ended up jammed into the cab, and when we tried to rearrange in the hotel parking lot, I hit my limit.

Let's just say Lori patiently talking me through repacking was not what I wanted in that moment. But it was a reminder that even with careful planning, there's always room for adjustments.

We'll do better on the return trip.

Enough is Freedom

Once we embraced the limits of our truck bed, packing

became easier. The constraints didn't feel restrictive — they felt freeing. The same applies to work, time, and even life.

What if we thought of our careers and commitments in the same way? What's truly necessary? What's just taking up space?

As I settle back into Indiana for the week, I find myself applying this question beyond just my belongings. What does it mean to pack light in how I approach my work, my relationships, my priorities? How much do I carry just because I always have?

Perhaps the lesson is this: clarity comes from defining what's enough — no more, no less.

And when we know what's enough, we move forward with intention.

Your Turn:

What are you carrying "just in case"?

What would it look like to repack this week — your schedule, your workspace, your obligations — with only what truly fits?

You Can't Take It With You (At Least for Now)

On snacks, space, and the stories we carry

At some point during our time here in Picture Rocks, I found myself standing in the fluorescent glow of the Speedway gas station, looking for trail mix. Not just any trail mix—Choco-Nut Trail Mix, the kind with the generic M&Ms, almonds, raisins, peanuts, and maybe something else that's only there for color or texture. It had become a small ritual, a modest joy, part of the winding-down routine on late afternoons when errands and heat had taken their toll.

But today, the basket where it usually sat was empty.

No big deal, I told myself. There's another store just across the intersection—two Speedway gas stations, same owner, kitty-corner to one another—a quirk of Picture Rocks that seems to match its name. It's not really a town, more like a long, sunbaked stretch of desert life, scattered RVs and single-wides, local characters, and cacti with more permanence than people.

Still, no trail mix.

I checked again the next day. Still nothing.

Now I was no longer casually looking. I was on a mission.

Somewhere between the third and fourth store visit, I realized I was fixated. The choco-nut trail mix had become the thing. A placeholder for whatever emotional craving I wasn't naming. I didn't want trail mix — I wanted something to land, something that made the day feel like it added up. It wasn't about hunger. It was about completion.

The Etiquette of the Mix

Meanwhile, back at the tiny house, Lori and I had started our low-stakes bickering routine. It had become a recurring bit: the etiquette of trail mix consumption.

Now, if you ask me (and I am obviously correct in this), trail mix is a contract. You don't cherry-pick the M&Ms or the chocolate pieces. You take what you get. No picking. No cheating. It's not a candy bowl. It's a mix. The magic is in the blend.

But lately, I'd reach into the bag and pull out only peanuts. Sometimes raisins. Never chocolate. And while I didn't want to accuse anyone, it became clear that my trail mix had been curated.

"I don't know what you're talking about," Lori would say, not quite convincingly.

"Just saying," I'd reply, shaking the bag. "No chocolate left. That's all I'm saying."

We were laughing, mostly. But also, there's something real in that tension. Something about what we take and what we leave — in food, in relationships, in daily choices.

The Weight of Small Things

We all have our version of trail mix. The thing we fixate on. The small, seemingly inconsequential item that holds a bigger emotional weight. Maybe it's a routine. A job title. A piece of gear. A past success. Or the idea that something — if we just had it — would make us feel a little more in control.

But here's the truth we keep running into out here in the

desert: You can't take it all with you. Not in a tiny house. Not in a marriage. Not in a day packed with too much. And certainly not into whatever future we imagine is waiting for us.

When we packed for Arizona, we followed The Rule of the Truck Bed: if it didn't fit in the bed of the Maverick, it didn't come. No trailer. No backup storage. Just what was needed for this leg of the journey.

And we've mostly stuck to it. But emotionally? That's harder. We carry things we think we need—resentments, expectations, fears, stories we're not quite ready to rewrite.

We pick out the chocolate and try to pretend we're still enjoying the mix.

This Is the Mix We've Got

Even Colin, home for part of his spring break, caught us mid-bicker over the trail mix. At some point, he just shook his head—maybe amused, maybe wondering how two grown adults could spend so much time debating snack protocol:

"Please don't discuss this anymore."

But he wasn't wrong. When you add a third person (and a cat) into 233 square feet of tiny house life, everything gets amplified—the footsteps, the schedules, the preferences, the snacks. Even our jokes take up space.

And yet, we make it work. Because this is the mix we've got.

Perhaps the real point isn't whether we got the chocolate or the peanuts or the last word. It's whether we can sit in a small space together and keep laughing. Keep adjusting. Keep showing up, even when the mix isn't perfect.

That's what the desert teaches, what the tiny house reinforces, and what I keep learning: you don't get to curate every detail. But if you can stay present with what remains—if you can learn to appreciate the parts you didn't choose—you might just find it's enough.

Maybe even more than enough.

Your Turn:

What are you fixating on right now that might really be about something else?

What would it mean to pause, accept the mix you've got, and stay present with what's already in front of you?

Of Cholla and Men

Not everything painful is without value

When we first walked the land where Casa Saguaro now stands, I wore shorts. I hadn't yet met the cholla.

I thought I understood the desert. I'd seen the postcards—the tall, symmetrical saguaros with their arms raised like gentle guardians of the Southwest. They're easy to draw, easy to love, and often the face of the desert in emoji form.

But the cholla? No emojis. No t-shirts. No trail guide reverence. Just pain.

The first time a cholla "jumped" onto my bare calf, I realized just how wrong I'd been. These weren't just prickly plants; they were the desert's reality check. As I later learned, the barbs are designed not just to pierce but to hold. Removal with your hands? Big mistake. I now carry a wide-toothed comb—yes, the banana comb from the 80s—to pry them off safely. A retro solution to a desert problem.

We were told by a neighbor that our land had likely never been cleared before—not in decades, maybe never. We inherited a thick tangle of native growth, with cholla dominating entire sections like barbed barricades.

Clearing and Burning

The cholla was the first thing I needed to clear to make way for our home. Cutting them down, piling the branches, and—after getting the proper fire permit—burning them. The neighbor-approved method? A propane torch, safer and more effective than the DIY attempts of my past (which may or may not have involved gasoline and poor judgment).

Before I learned the safer way, I tried hauling full tarps of chopped cholla across the property with a rope and an electric saw, wearing gloves that weren't thick enough and sleeves that weren't long enough.

But burning isn't just about removal. It's about making space. It's about confronting what's painful and inconvenient—not to erase it, but to understand its limits and purpose.

What the Saguaro Gets and the Cholla Doesn't

The saguaro is revered. It has stories, symmetry, and spiritual associations. The cholla is… avoided. And yet, both are native. Both are vital. The cholla provides cover for doves. Its barbed segments become building material for pack rats—desert engineers who've been at this longer than any of us.

There's a danger in simplifying the landscape into good and bad, beautiful and bothersome. Some things don't fit our aesthetic or our plans—but they serve a purpose. They've adapted. And sometimes, they ask us to do the same.

In one area of our land, we left the cholla alone. It's now where we regularly see quail darting through, a whole network of animal life thriving where we once saw only hazard.

Land, Value, and the Things We Dismiss

I'm conscious of the impact. A friend back in Indiana asked me, "What's the ecological consequence of clearing the cholla?" And they were right to ask. It made me pause.

Because clearing isn't just about removal. It's about intention. And while we've left space for wildlife and native plants, the lesson remains: Not everything painful is without value. Not everything wild needs taming.

Even here in Picture Rocks, a place some call "lawless" or "the Wild West," there are permits, boundaries, community respect. Even fire has to be negotiated with care.

And maybe that's the reminder: not everything sharp or stubborn is meant to be removed. Sometimes it's there to teach us how to stay, how to listen, how to live with complexity.

Your Turn:

What part of your life are you trying to clear that might still serve a purpose?

Where might you be invited to live with complexity instead of erasing it?

The Tiny House and the Fog

The Fog I Built—and the Home That Cleared It

The Illusion of Expertise

Years ago, I was deep into a chess phase—not competing, not training, but consuming. I'd walk into bookstores and head straight for the games shelf: *How to Play Good Opening Moves*, *Chess: Tactics and Strategies*, *The Most Instructive Games of Chess Ever Played*, *Reassess Your Chess* (workbook), and the partial set of Garry Kasparov on *My Great Predecessors* (Volumes 1–5) — I bought them all.

Not because I was studying them. But because I liked what they represented.

They weren't the only books I collected.

There was the stack of programming manuals I never coded from. The shelf of leadership texts I never annotated. The volumes of Latin primers, teaching strategy guides, and dusty theological tomes I didn't so much read as arrange. Together, they formed a kind of curated projection: a library not of mastery, but of intention. A portrait of the expert I wanted others to assume I already was.

It felt productive. Almost noble.

But really, it was a well-organized fog.

What I was chasing wasn't growth—it was identity. Or at

least, the appearance of it. And the more I surrounded myself with those titles, the more I mistook proximity for fluency.

This wasn't a hunger for depth. It was a fear of not knowing enough. And instead of clarity, I got clutter.

The Weight of Too Much

My time in the desert—at Casa Saguaro, where the tiny house lives among the quail, cholla, desert wrens, and the occasional curious coyote—was a kind of transition.

For seven years, I'd worked in a position that centered on coaching teachers. I'd observe classrooms, offer feedback, and help shape instruction to align with larger goals. That work often brought me face to face with pacing guides—local, state, national—that tried to do everything: every writing mode, every reading skill, every test target. Nothing could be left behind.

Even in my current contract work during these desert months, the story hasn't changed much. I still find myself reviewing state standards and curriculum maps that aim to cover it all. There's a quiet pressure there, one that builds up like sand in a boot: teachers feel like they have to "cover" everything, "teach" everything. But at what cost?

And what about the students?

Are they tracking all of these targets? Or are they, too, buried beneath the weight of expectations they never asked for?

I'd come home to our tiny house—every square inch accounted for—and unpack the day while slipping off my shoes at the door. Maybe I'd set down something new I'd ordered off Amazon. A book. A tool. A kitchen gadget. And Lori would ask, not unkindly:

"Okay, where's that going to go?"

That question grounded me.

Because it wasn't just about space. It was about purpose. If something came in, something else had to go. If we didn't know where it would live, it didn't belong.

Meanwhile, in schools, we kept adding. More standards. More systems. More strategies. And almost never asking:

"Where does that go?"

If our homes can't handle excess without tension, why do we expect our classrooms to?

Living With Less, On Purpose

This is why the Tiny House metaphor keeps showing up for me—not just in teaching, but in how I try to live and lead.

It's not about asceticism or trend-chasing. It's about design. About limits that sharpen purpose.

In a tiny house, you don't keep every book—you keep the ones you actually read. The ones you return to. You don't arrange a life to look impressive. You arrange it to function.

It applies in every role we hold.

Leaders? Clear space for clarity, not control.

Parents? Choose connection over activity.

Writers? Trade productivity for presence.

The Tiny House isn't about less for the sake of less. It's about honest alignment—between who we are and what we carry.

So maybe the question isn't "What could I add?"

Maybe it's: "What have I already carried too long?"

Because once the fog lifts, the essentials feel like air again.

The Shelf Doesn't Have to Be Full

I started this post with a quiet confession: I want it all. Like the Queen lyric—*I want it all, and I want it now.*

That desire doesn't come from ego. I think it comes from the anxiety of missing something important. That if I just had one more book, one more strategy, one more piece of information— I'd be ready.

But most of us aren't suffering from a lack of input. We're just trying to breathe through the smog.

David Shenk named it back in the 90s: *Data Smog* — a fog of good intentions, where more content becomes less clarity. And in our classrooms, our inboxes, our libraries, and our lives, we keep inhaling it, hoping something will click.

But maybe clarity doesn't come from reaching for more. Maybe it comes from reaching for less, on purpose.

So here's the handoff:

What would it look like this week to live just one step closer to the tiny house?

Not to throw everything out — but to carry less with more care.

Not to prove you're fluent — but to show up with focus.

The shelf doesn't have to be full to say something meaningful.

Your Turn:

What are you holding onto that looks like progress — but might actually be fog?

What would it take to clear space — for clarity, not for show?

On the Road, Still

Speed limits, desert roads, and the permission to linger

Out here in Picture Rocks, the roads teach patience.

Every drive starts with a choice: dirt or paved, bumps or smooth, thirty miles per hour or something slower. On West Rudasill, the posted limit is twenty-five—though it feels like there should be more. The road opens wide, the desert stretches out forever, and still the sign insists: 25.

Locals will tell you it's not for the tourists or the traffic—it's for the people who live here. For the kids walking a dog, the neighbor pulling out of a gravel driveway, the one who waves from behind a cloud of dust. The sign isn't a rule so much as a reminder: someone lives here. Someone's watching.

A mile later, it shifts to thirty. Then, eventually, forty.

It's funny how the landscape decides the pace—closer houses mean slower speed; open spaces invite acceleration. Even the asphalt seems to change personality depending on who lives beside it.

On the dirt roads, though, there are no posted limits. The rain carves tiny ribs across the surface, turning every stretch into a washboard. You learn quickly that slow isn't always safe. At fifteen miles an hour, the truck rattles like a shopping cart. At thirty, it suddenly glides. Too slow, and you feel every bump. Too fast, and you lose control. Somewhere between the two, the shocks do their work, and the ride becomes bearable.

There's a strange poetry in that: sometimes speeding up is what steadies you.

...

I think about that when I remember our family's long tradition of leaving early.

Every Fourth of July, we'd start the slow exit from the park right as the fireworks started to wind down. We'd tell the kids, "We'll see them from the car." We'd roll down the windows, crane our necks, try to catch the finale between streetlights and treetops—all so we could "beat the traffic."

But of course, we never really did.

We just joined a different kind of crowd—everyone else trying to escape the same moment.

What we missed wasn't the fireworks. It was the permission to stay—to linger through the noise and smoke, to let wonder finish its sentence before moving on.

And yet, we do it everywhere.

At concerts, lectures, church services, even dinners with friends—we start packing up before the ending arrives. We're halfway out the door of our own lives, planning our escape from now.

...

Maybe that's why the desert feels like correction.

It won't let you rush. The roads resist. The curves around Picture Rocks demand attention, the washboard hum keeps you grounded in the moment. Out here, hurry feels foreign, almost impolite.

Driving through this place, you start to wonder: what if speed limits aren't about safety so much as sanity? What if they're not meant to restrain us but to rescue us from our own momentum?

Every road out here carries its own pace.

And maybe that's the invitation—to notice the road you're on and match it, not fight it.

Your Turn:

Where are you tempted to leave early—emotionally, mentally, or physically?

What might open up if you chose to stay, even just a little longer?

The Hunger Games (and the Leftovers)

The Sonoran hot dog is not the problem (probably)

We're still having a conversation about our refrigerator out here in the desert—how much do we really need? Or maybe more honestly: how much actually fits into the half-sized fridge that came with the tiny house?

It's not just the fridge. The washer, dryer, bathroom sink— everything here is scaled down. Even the shower is a pleasant surprise: tall enough for me to stand under without hunching like a crypt keeper. Storage space? Turns out, we have enough. Clothes, dry goods, dishes (not enough for a dinner party, but we've accepted that parties of eight are... unlikely, for now). Even Neko the cat has his own private cabinet for his litter box. Credit where it's due: Lori's been the architect of this quiet sufficiency. She shops and organizes with a clear question in mind—what do we actually need?

And all is well. Until Thursday grocery day.

That's when the fridge becomes a negotiation. What will fit? What do we have room for in the freezer? And inevitably, I'll let out a small whine: *"I don't have anything to eat."*

Now, to be fair, our boys are off living their own lives, and Lori and I often cook for ourselves. Her diet's more plant-based, more thoughtful, more...well, reduced. She finishes things. Even old coffee. She was built for tiny house living.

Me? I'm built for just-in-case scenarios. My backpack is a disaster kit: allergy meds, spare vitamins, backup mask, hat, underwear (because what if I'm in an accident?), and snacks. Always snacks. There's even a lint roller in the glove box. Just in case.

So I shouldn't be surprised that when I bemoan our dinner options, what I'm really craving isn't food—it's something shiny. New. Exciting. The burrito from Nico's. The Sonoran hot dog from the taco truck. Anything but leftovers. Anything but *planned*.

And that's when Lori drops a line that sticks: *"I think you have food anxiety."*

At first, I push back. I'm not anxious. I'm *prepared*. But when I sit with it—really sit—I can feel the truth: it's not just about food. It's about *enoughness*.

I like the first day of things. The thrill of novelty. The illusion of abundance. I'm drawn to the beginning—and not always great at sticking around after that.

I remember being on a studio tour in L.A. as a teenager, seeing the *Leave It to Beaver* house and the ominous Bates house from *Psycho*. Both of those houses had meant a lot to me growing up. I watched the Beav and Wally and their parents navigate life in the black-and-white 1950s—Wally's classic big brother shrug in response to Eddie Haskell's constant ribbing still sticks with me: "He's just giving you the business."

And then there was *Psycho*—the ultimate Hitchcock film. A story of mothers and sons and the women who got in the way. Creepy, brilliant, unforgettable.

Now here I was, riding past the real houses, the actual backlot structures. Except, of course, they weren't real. They looked complete from the front, but walk around back and there were no kitchens, no hallways, no place for June to serve dinner or Norman to brood in the attic. Just façades. Partial shells made to seem whole.

That's stuck with me. Because in my life, I've built façades too—intentions without plans, promises without timelines. I've craved the feeling of readiness without doing the work of commitment. The tiny house, in contrast, is the real deal: there's a kitchen, a place to sleep, a place to clean up. And yes, a fridge. Not big, but *real*.

So now, in the desert, I'm trying to live differently.

To see limitations not as punishments, but as clarity.
To sit with what's already in the fridge.
To stop mistaking shiny for sacred.
To remember that the leftovers are still food.
That the promise is still mine to keep.

Your Turn:

Where are you still reaching for something new instead of noticing what's already in the fridge?

What part of your life has become a façade—and what would it take to build something livable?

Reduce Wrap (Tiny House / Turn)

You've practiced letting go.
Or holding on with a little more care.
Maybe now you see what fits.
Maybe you've noticed what doesn't need to come with you.
What shifted when you carried less?
What cleared when you let one thing go?
The space is still there.
You can return to it anytime.
You don't have to carry it all.

Persist

The way forward is often not fast. But it is ours. One step, then another, then another.

PERSIST: Tom Made Me Do It

Persist — The Marathon

On running, rhythm, and learning to stay with the long work.

Tom asked if I wanted to run a half marathon, and I said, "Sure."

He sent me a twelve-week training plan. I did the last four.

I finished, but I was injured. Wrong shoes—you're supposed to go a size up; feet swell. What I thought was a knee injury turned out to be an IT band issue, the kind that teaches you humility faster than any coach could.

At the post-race celebration, Tom, grinning , asked if we should do a full marathon next.

Even though I was still limping, I said yes. Maybe Chicago.

The next year, I ran that same half again, then the Lakefront Marathon in Wisconsin. I finished. Less injured this time.

Somewhere in those miles, I stopped being someone who "tried running" and quietly became a runner.

…

What hooked me wasn't speed or medals. It was rhythm.

Training gave the days shape. Tuesdays were tempo runs; Thursdays, intervals; Sundays, long miles that started in darkness and ended with the sunrise.

I tried the Hanson Brothers plan—the runners, not the

singers—where the longest run is only sixteen miles, but the week itself is heavier. Two SOS runs: "Something of Substance."

Speedwork. Tempo runs. Accumulated fatigue that teaches your body to run on tired legs.

It worked. My times improved, but more than that, I started to learn running itself.

The first six miles are for silence—getting out of your head, finding the rhythm.

After that, you settle into a liminal space between effort and ease, a moving meditation that lasts until fatigue reintroduces you to yourself around mile eighteen.

That's when the inner committee convenes: Why are you doing this? You could stop. You could walk. You could lie down and moan in the middle of the road.

But you don't. You keep going.

You focus on your breath, the sound of shoes against pavement, the next visible thing—a tree, a turn, a volunteer with a cup of water.

Sometimes you smile for thirty seconds just to change the chemistry. Sometimes you high-five a kid on the curb.

And somewhere in that mix of exhaustion and grace, you find yourself moving forward again.

...

The desert has changed my pace.

In Indiana, I ran through seasons—cold, snow, wind, ice.

In the Sonoran heat, there's no rhythm yet. The calendar doesn't guide you; the sun does. Some days, I start before dawn; others, I let the heat win and stay home.

I'm slower now. I stretch more. I do yoga.

And still, I run.

Not to prove anything, but to stay connected—to the body, to the moment, to whatever small thing keeps me honest.

Out here, the landscape teaches patience. A rabbit darts across the trail. A turtle crosses slowly, deliberate as prayer. Sometimes those encounters feel like little haiku: unexpected, quiet, true.

I used to think persistence was about finishing faster.

Now, I know it's about returning.

Returning to the trail. Returning to yourself. Returning to the small promise that still feels worth keeping.

...

Practice Invitation — Circles of Change

Name one small shift you want to make.

Track it for a while. Let it unfold.

Persistence doesn't always look heroic.

Sometimes it's just one more mile, one more breath, one more gentle yes.

Zen and the Art of Water Heater Maintenance

Staying present with the work right in front of you.

Not everyone on our "what it's like to live in a Tiny House in Tucson" tour wants the full explanation. Maybe that's just me — I like telling the whole story. And, if this first stretch of living in Casa Saguaro has taught me anything, it's that every small victory comes with a new challenge. Just when we get one thing fixed, another thing reminds us that we're still in transition.

That first month, it was the electricity. Then, the plumbing. By the time we reached a point where things were stable, Lori and I started bickering. I think we were both waiting for normal to settle in, but every small win seemed to bring a new setback.

The Return to The Estate & The Rotten Egg Smell

Back in Indiana for a week, stepping into The Estate, Lori pointed something out as soon as we walked in:

"What is that smell?"

It wasn't just the musty scent of a house closed up for weeks — it was something sulfuric, like rotten eggs. I mentally added it to my to-do list, but my focus was already on the pump house and the well pipes that had burst while we were gone.

The next morning, I smelled it again every time we turned on the hot water. I read the directions on fixing it, but I didn't act right away. Maybe I thought it would just go away. Maybe I didn't want to deal with one more problem. Either way, Lori sent me a link explaining how to remove the smell, and I finally started paying attention.

The House We Built (and the One We Thought Would Arrive)

The Estate was never meant to exist. It was supposed to be a temporary stop—a place to live while we waited for the tiny house we had ordered. But after delays and supply chain issues, we reached a point where we had a choice: keep waiting, or build something ourselves.

I didn't think I had the skill set for a remodel, but with some encouragement (and a bit of necessity), I took the gutted mobile home down to its frame and started over. Insulating, re-studding, replumbing the entire thing. The water heater that now smelled like rotten eggs? I had installed that myself. And now, it was giving us problems.

"How old is the water heater?" Lori asked.

"New with the remodel."

"Where did the old one go?"

I smiled. She already knew the answer. I had moved the old one out by myself, and it didn't sit there long before a neighbor stopped by.

"You want that?" I asked.

"Absolutely."

Within hours, he was back with his truck, probably stripping it for scrap metal. I could have done the same, but sometimes it's better to let go of what no longer serves you.

Problem-Solving is a Marathon, Not a Sprint

So now I was standing in front of my "new" water heater, ready to fix the smell. I had the instructions. I had the tools. I even made a trip to Dollar General to pick up unscented bleach and a long funnel, thinking I was about to follow the standard steps:

1. Turn off the breaker.
2. Shut off the incoming water.
3. Drain the 50-gallon tank.
4. Clean everything out.

But before I started, I checked the online manual. Was there another way?

And there it was: "If you experience a sulfur smell, turn up the temperature to 140°F to kill off the bacteria."

No draining. No bleach. Just adjusting a setting and letting the system take care of itself. I turned the dial, let the heater run, and sure enough—the smell faded. A small adjustment solved the problem.

Pacing, Adjustment, and Trusting the Process

On my run that afternoon, I noticed something familiar. The Pumpkinvine Trail seemed the same but different. I had only taken a few days off, but I could feel it in my legs. The first mile was slow, but by the second mile, I was back in rhythm. That's how running works. That's how problem-solving works.

I used to get impatient with my own runs, wanting to push through discomfort too soon. But after years of training, I've learned that you have to warm up, adjust, and let the process unfold.

Fixing the water heater wasn't about finding a perfect solution right away. It was about stepping into the process, reading, adjusting, and trusting that forward motion would get me there.

Lessons from Water Heaters and Running Trails

Not every problem requires an extreme solution. Sometimes, small adjustments work better than a complete overhaul.

Patience and process matter. Whether it's training for a marathon, fixing a house, or adjusting to change, we have to trust that momentum builds over time.

We don't have to do everything the hardest way possible. Sometimes, we overcomplicate things just because we assume they should be difficult. What if we just checked the manual first?

Maybe that's the lesson for today: Some fixes don't come from force—they come from understanding what's really needed and giving it time to work.

Your Turn:

What small adjustment could you make today instead of a full overhaul?

Where might patience solve what pressure cannot?

The Warren and the Wide World: Writing Between Safety and Discovery

What happens when the work asks you to leave your burrow and go a little farther

It's funny what you notice when your routines break down.

Before we left for Arizona, I had a rhythm: mornings at Starbucks, afternoons writing, evenings winding down. Nothing glamorous, nothing earth-shattering, just a steady, familiar cycle.

Then came the move. New place, new routines—or, more accurately, no routines at all. And with that, a strange kind of drift set in.

It's not that I wasn't working. I was still writing. Still showing up.

But without the anchor of routine, everything felt harder.

Routines Aren't Glamorous, But They Are Powerful

There's a myth we sometimes buy into—that creativity should feel spontaneous, electric, driven by sudden bursts of inspiration.

But the truth is, most of the meaningful work gets done by showing up in ordinary ways, over and over again.

Writing a blog post. Drafting a new program. Planning a session.

None of it requires fireworks.

It requires habit.

When routines are in place, they remove one big obstacle: decision fatigue.

You don't have to ask yourself whether you'll write today. You already know.

The question becomes simpler: What will you write today?

Routine Is Like Marathon Training

When I trained for marathons, I didn't wake up full of energy every day.

Some days, my legs felt like concrete. Some days, I wanted to turn around after the first mile.

But the rhythm of the training plan—not my mood—carried me forward.

It wasn't about how I felt at mile one.

It was about trusting that if I showed up, if I stayed in motion, my body would find the rhythm it knew how to keep.

Writing—and really, any meaningful work—is the same.

Routine builds resilience, not just results.

You don't have to feel good to make progress. You have to trust the process enough to keep moving.

When Routine Slips, So Does Flow

During those early Arizona days, I noticed how quickly the absence of routine unraveled everything else.

Writing sessions got shorter.

Focus came slower.

Momentum faded.

It's like a long-distance run—you don't lose fitness all at once. You lose it gradually, quietly, without realizing until you're struggling halfway through a mile that used to feel easy.

The same happens with creative flow.

Without consistent rhythms, it's easy to confuse discomfort for inability.

It's easy to wonder, Am I just bad at this?

But it's not ability that's lacking. It's structure.

Tiny Shifts Rebuild Big Routines

The solution wasn't glamorous either.

It was getting back to basics:

Returning to a set morning time to write (even if it felt clumsy at first)

- Sitting in the same chair
- Making coffee the same way
- Opening the same draft file

Small signals to the brain:

We are doing this again. We are moving forward.

It didn't feel magical right away. But step by step, the flow returned.

Not because inspiration struck—but because routine made space for discovery.

A Word About Personality and Routine

As an Enneagram 7, routine has not always been my natural ally.

I crave spontaneity, newness, adventure. A structured plan can feel like a cage to my instinct for exploration.

But what running—and writing—have taught me is that routine doesn't have to kill spontaneity. In fact, routine can make space for it.

When you're out on a familiar running trail, it's not the

predictability that keeps you going. It's the unexpected—a rabbit darting across the path, a sudden breeze, a new shade of light at sunset—that reminds you you're alive and moving through a wide, open world.

Routine sets the stage. Magic shows up when you're already in motion.

A Final Thought: Routines Are Rescue Boats, Not Cages

A lot of writers and teachers (myself included) sometimes bristle at the idea of strict routines.

They can feel limiting, dull, rigid.

But good routines aren't cages.

They're rescue boats.

They carry us through the mornings when inspiration doesn't show up.

They give us a rhythm to trust when the work feels heavy.

They remind us that consistency builds confidence, even when the page is blank.

So if you're struggling today—not with ability, but with momentum—maybe don't ask, What should I create today?

Maybe ask, Where can I rebuild a routine that makes creating feel possible again?

One small rhythm at a time.

Your Turn:

What routine helps you return to your work when inspiration fades?
How might structure make more room for surprise?

89

When Things Fall Apart (and So Do We)

On stepping back, resetting the rhythm, and rebuilding what still matters

Burnout doesn't usually arrive with fireworks.

It comes quietly—like a late fee you forgot to pay or a cold creeping into your throat. Subtle at first. A missed run. An unopened book. A skipped writing session. Then suddenly, it's been a week—or more—and you're left wondering how you drifted so far off course.

This is a post about that drift.

There are plenty of metaphors for burnout, but the one I keep returning to is heat exhaustion. I've trained in the desert. I've run through Indiana humidity. And here's what I've learned: push too long without rest, and the crash is inevitable. You can't power through it. Your body will shut down. Your mind follows.

At the Starbucks I call my home office, I've noticed Tucson is a training town. You hear it in the small talk—CrossFit schedules, early morning runs, desert hikes. Recently, I overheard a pair of younger athletes:

"Rest days are for wimps."

I may have nodded along once, in younger years when pushing through was a badge of honor. But now? I know better.

Rest isn't weakness. It's wisdom. It's a strategy. It's the pause between notes that makes music—not just relentless sound. That's why the Pomodoro principle—bursts of focused work followed by rest—feels so counterintuitive, but works so well. It respects rhythm. It trusts recovery.

Much like the traditional Sabbath, rest invites us to embrace our limits. It reminds us: we're not machines. The best endurance, whether in training or teaching or writing, comes not from constant effort, but from the balance between action and recovery.

That's what I've been learning again.

Because I've fallen off before. I'll fall off again. But this time, I'm noticing the signs sooner. I'm giving myself space to pause—before the crash.

Here's what I'm trying:

- A skipped day isn't the end. It's an invitation to begin again.

- A reset doesn't mean failure. It means noticing what's not working.

- A tired body isn't laziness. It's information.

Some seasons ask more of us.

Some days drain us faster than expected.

But if we listen—really listen—to the body, to the pace, to the pull of our work and rest, we can begin again. With care. With clarity. With better pacing.

And most of all? I'm learning that growth isn't about never falling apart—it's about knowing how to rebuild.

Maybe that's the real gift of the marathon mindset:

Not the speed—but the staying.

Even when things fall apart.

Even when we do.

We begin again.

Your Turn:

What would happen if you treated rest as part of the work rather than its opposite?

Where could you pause before you push?

A Farewell to Ladders: Much Ado About Fastening

What building a deck taught me about fluency, patience, and why it's okay to stay in gear one—for a while.

Setting the Last Screw (Almost)

Ten screws short. Out of 374, just ten left to go. That's where I found myself—hands dusty, knees sore, the new deck on our tiny house almost complete. And with that, the first phase of this new chapter in tiny living came to a close.

The deck was more than a platform. It was a canvas, a structure marking the transition from just getting by to having a functional, livable space. It was drawn up by my brother-in-law—a structural engineer whose thesis was literally on concrete—and it was solid. His plans were like old-school schematics: follow view A, then view B. Stick to the blueprint, and you'll be okay.

But, of course, nothing ever goes exactly as drawn.

Learning by Doing (and Asking)

I didn't grow up with tools in my hand. My mom used to pay

the neighbor kid (my best friend) to mow our lawn. And yet, here I was, 374 screws deep into a deck I had built with my own hands. It wasn't my first project. Years ago, I rebuilt a porch and a deck with borrowed advice and borrowed tools. I learned to cut spindles, reinforce joints. Four years ago, I redid the gutted "Estate" and even found out what PEX plumbing was—life-changing, by the way.

This time, I leaned on muscle memory and phone calls. I borrowed a chop saw from my neighbor Ken, who kindly gave me a 45-minute unsolicited inspection and advice session. Some of it was practical (how to clamp a warped board), some of it was life story (his old shop in Florida), but all of it was welcome.

His parting feedback stuck: "It's not level. But it's solid." I'll take that.

Two Gears, One Lesson

Now here's the part where a drill becomes a teacher.

On my power drill, there are two settings. One is slow and steady. The other is fast but harder to control. For most of the build, I stayed in gear one—safe, predictable, but slow. Eventually, I tried gear two. The drill bucked, the screw heads stripped. I wasn't ready. But after about 75 tries, I figured it out: line it up slow, then press through. It wasn't speed that made it work. It was rhythm, and eventually, feel.

That moment reminded me of writing.

So often we ask students to write as if they're already in gear two—fast, polished, precise. But most haven't even learned how to hold the drill yet. We give them rubrics before they've built anything. We assess final products when what they need is permission to practice, strip a few screws, and keep going.

The Plateau of Progress

Writing, like construction, like living, takes repetition. You line it up. You engage. You notice. You repeat. And every so often, you reflect. That's where growth happens—not in the product, but in the doing.

We ask this of runners, of musicians, of artists. Why not of writers?

In his book *Mastery*, George Leonard writes about the plateau—the long, flat stretch of effort where there's little visible progress but deep development is happening. Mastery, he argues, isn't about constant improvement. It's about learning to love the plateau. To stay with the work when it feels slow and quiet, and to trust that something is being built even when you can't yet see it.

And that's the work of writing. Of teaching. Of building anything that lasts.

The Deck, and the Invitation

I did go back and drill in those last ten screws. And with that, the deck was finished. A few weeks earlier, we were using a step ladder just to get into our front door—awkward, temporary, always a bit precarious. Now, with the deck in place, it's not just an improvement; it's an extension of our tiny house living. It's where we now drink coffee, hold conversations, and end our days.

What was once a rough workaround is now part of the structure. And we've already forgotten what it felt like not to have it.

That's the quiet beauty of repetition and rhythm—of staying in gear one long enough to build something real. And maybe that's the invitation, too.

Not just for ourselves, but for others: to give space for slow starts, uneven progress, and gradual confidence. To trust that fluency follows practice. That over time, what feels like effort becomes ease—and what once felt temporary becomes part of how we live and work.

Your Turn:

What skill or habit deserves another slow repetition?

How might you stay with the practice long enough to feel its ease return?

The Play's the Thing (Even When You Lose the Queen)

On setbacks, endurance, and the next move we can still make

Evan and I have played chess together since he was barely out of toddlerhood. I have a photo of him, maybe three years old, already knowing how to move the knight—the horsey, as he called it. That early joy launched years of games. Tournaments, wins, losses. Sometimes he beat me; sometimes I held my own. But always, we came back to the board. Because it wasn't about ranking or mastery. It was about the practice. About what the game invites you to see.

Recently we played online. I made a move that took his queen. I didn't do it recklessly—he had a knight that could take me back. I figured he'd see it, trade the knight for the queen, and the game would continue. But he didn't see it. And he resigned. Just like that. I remember messaging him: "Dude, you shouldn't have resigned. It wasn't over."

Because it wasn't. The board was still there. Pieces still in play. But the moment felt too big. The setback felt like the end, because in chess, if you lose your most powerful piece–the Queen–all seems lost.

And isn't that how it goes? Setbacks feel final when you're in them.

I see it in myself. Take my running shoes, for example. I've run for years, and like anyone in a sport, you find yourself getting attached to certain gear. For me, it wasn't about flashy outfits — most of my race shirts came from the events themselves — but shoes were a different story. I learned early, after some painful missteps, that long-distance running isn't kind to shoes that don't fit right. My first marathon taught me that lesson the hard way: I needed shoes at least a half size bigger to accommodate swelling. So I went to a proper running store, learned about gait and pronation, and settled on Asics. A stable, reliable shoe that served me well for over a decade. Same model, year after year. I'd write the date on the side of the shoe to track when it was time for a new pair — about every 500 miles or so. And then, they changed the model. The fit wasn't right anymore. Too tight. I don't have especially wide feet, but they felt wrong. I switched brands — now I run in Brooks — but every so often, I look at Asics again, wondering if I can just get back to that perfect fit. That if I could, everything else would click too.

And then there's the Gatorade bottles. I used to rely on those 24-ounce sport cap bottles for my long runs. Not because I'm a big Gatorade fan — I'd usually dump out the drink and fill the bottle with water — but because the size was perfect. The grip, the cap, the durability. They'd last me an entire season for just a couple bucks. But lately, I couldn't find them. I checked every gas station, every convenience store, and eventually turned to Amazon, where I ended up with a strap but no bottle. It felt absurd, how much energy I was spending trying to replace this small, familiar tool. Then, one day back in Indiana, I spotted a single bottle on a bottom shelf at a gas station. I grabbed it without hesitation. The next time I stopped in, they had a whole row of them, and I bought two — just two — because Lori gently reminded me not to start hoarding. A kind reminder that the comfort of familiar things can turn quickly into clinging.

But here's the realization that keeps returning — because life keeps making me relearn it.

I've written before about the trail mix I hoarded on hikes, as if carrying more would protect me. About the Indiana weather I grumbled about, as if complaining would change it. I named those moments. I tried to draw lessons from them. And yet, here I am again. Shouldn't I have learned that by now? Shouldn't writing about it have sealed the wisdom in place? When I find myself grasping again, or complaining again, doesn't that mean I've failed?

That's the trick the mind plays. The voice that says: You should have mastered this already. That frames every setback as weakness, every lapse as proof of character flaw. That whispers: If you were strong enough, you wouldn't need to relearn. And so the stumble isn't just a human moment—it becomes shame. The internal voice flails: You're weak. You fell off the wagon. You failed.

It's the same voice behind New Year's resolutions. The one that says habits are binary: you're either winning or you're not. That if you slip, you might as well quit. And it hurts—not just the slip itself, but the judgment we pile on top.

But that isn't how life works. The world doesn't run on streaks. The chess game with Evan reminds me: the setback feels massive. The queen is gone. All is lost—or so it seems. But the board is still there. The game isn't over. The loss is part of it. The unexpected, the humbling, the hard moments—they're part of it.

Maybe that's the deeper truth. Life isn't about keeping a perfect chain of wins, or habits, or good weather, or smooth runs. Setbacks don't signal failure. Victories don't buy immunity. The monsoon at Casa Saguaro isn't good or bad—it's rain. The humidity in Indiana isn't punishment—it's what makes things green.

And I think of *Chess: The Musical*—that concept album I was introduced to in Jeff's dorm room in 1985. Tim Rice and his team revised it again and again. After thirty or so years of versions, they could finally say, "I think at last we're getting it right."

Maybe that's the point. Not perfection, not over-optimism — but the steady work of staying in the game.

Maybe the task is to stop sorting everything into good and bad, success and failure. Maybe it's simply to notice: This is it. This is the present moment. Not as proof of worth or weakness, but as part of the rhythm. Ebb and flow. Sun and storm. Shoes that fit, and shoes that don't. Queens lost, and games still worth playing.

And maybe it's not about fixing or qualifying or labeling. Maybe it's about saying less. Expecting less of perfection. And living in this imperfect, still-beautiful present.

Your Turn:

What setback could you see as part of the pattern rather than its end?
When have you mistaken losing ground for losing heart?

All Quiet on the Desert Front

On solitude, entitlement, and learning to stay in the long work.

It rained last night in Picture Rocks.

A downpour, if you believe the sarcasm.

In Indiana, rain is measured in tenths of an inch —.1, .23, maybe a solid .6 on a good day. Here in the desert, it's a proud .01. Sparse. Reluctant. But it did smell like rain around 3 a.m. when I made my way downstairs, and the puddles on the truck bed cover said it happened.

That's desert rain for you. It never really soaks—it hints. Until monsoon season, when the ground can't take too much of a good thing and washes over in a rush, flooding out every low spot with water and hubris.

Later that morning, I made my usual trip to Starbucks. Lori was in Indiana for the week. I'd nudged her to go—partly because of the AC repair ordeal, partly because of the slow replies from family had her needing some time with old rhythms. And partly, if I'm honest, because I was tunnel-focused on catching up on projects. We had four weeks left at Casa Saguaro, and I felt the clock ticking.

At Starbucks, I noticed two guys doing what bros do—loud goodbyes, casual back-pats, the choreography of connection. And I realized something: in the four months we'd been here, I hadn't found my own bro.

Sure, I had text threads and Zoom calls with people who

matter. But the face-to-face, spontaneous community—the kind you build over drinks, side comments, and accidental run-ins—wasn't part of this season. We'd spent this stretch focused on finding our place in the wilderness, making polite conversation in lines, being present for each other and Neko. And maybe that was enough for now.

Still, I hoped Lori would see what I saw in her trip back to Indiana—that our roots there are still real, and that when we return to the desert, maybe we'll have more bandwidth to look up and build a wider circle. Maybe even find a bro for Chris.

But somewhere beneath that quiet longing, I've noticed another, less flattering layer.

Entitlement.

It sneaks in with small demands. Why does this task inconvenience me? Why do I have to jump through hoops for a contract that's remote? Why do I need a TB test when I'll never set foot in the building? Why a signed Social Security card when they can verify me with a click? (Which, of course, they can't, because the website is glitchy and my last physical SS card is probably buried in a high school memory box somewhere.)

The longer I sat with those irritations, the more I recognized them for what they were—not logistical grievances, but posturing. The subtle, creeping belief that I deserve a say in how things should go. That my expertise should exempt me from inconvenience. That I'm somehow above the bureaucratic noise.

It's not a far leap from there to waving a metaphorical "Karen/Ken" flag, insisting on speaking my mind on things that don't require my opinion.

That's the plank. And it's ugly when you see it.

I've spent years framing my work as service. As contribution. But apparently, there are strings attached to my generosity. Conditions to my kindness. I serve… until it gets frustrating. I contribute… until it's inconvenient. And I love… with a quiet expectation of being acknowledged for it.

Good to know. Better to remember.

There's no clever wrap-up here.

Just a reminder that the rain isn't obliged to impress me.

That the bro-goodbyes I watched aren't an indictment of my solitude.

That bureaucracy isn't a personal offense.

It's just life. Slow, repetitive, sometimes ridiculous.

Like a desert drizzle that still smells sweet at 3 a.m.

Like a road crew that builds inch by inch, day by day.

And maybe the real work is to stay in the long game of humility.

One .01 inch at a time.

Your Turn:

What expectation could you release to rediscover humility?

Where might quiet attention teach more than control?

A Kind of Homegoing

On leaving Casa Saguaro, tending to the ordinary work of departure, and learning how presence lingers even as we go

We have two weeks left at Casa Saguaro, though it hardly feels that long. Jan will visit this weekend, then we'll fly east for Jen and Nathan's graduation, and after that the long drive back to Indiana begins. It all feels both sudden and slow, as if time itself is stretching between lists.

Today is our thirty-fifth anniversary. Lori is at the tiny house finishing paint along the trim, and I'm at Starbucks six miles away, doing what I always do—writing, watching people. A group nearby, dressed for something formal, shares quiet laughter before piling into a white Wagoneer. In the corner, an older man tells a younger one he'll "walk through the fire with him." I half-listen, half-wonder if he means it.

Meanwhile our own fire is ordinary: the small, steady kind that lives inside tasks. The to-do list hums—paint the front door, fix the back-door lock, box what goes north, shut off what stays behind, secure the things that might fly away in a desert gust. Each check mark feels like both progress and rehearsal.

It's strange how endings echo beginnings. We make plans, rearrange furniture, measure the weight of what to keep. We tell ourselves we're getting ready, when what we're really doing is holding on. Maybe that's what leaving teaches us: the difference between readiness and presence.

The desert never tells you it's almost time to go.

You just start noticing small things—the paint chipped near the entryway, the squeak in the sliding door, the sag of a curtain rod that's been slightly off since February. The kind of things you'd ignored when you first arrived, because you were busy arriving.

Now you're busy leaving.

The mornings are slower, the to-do lists stranger. The house smells like cleaner and moving bins. I keep finding little piles of screws and tape, ghost traces of projects I swore I'd finish "before we left."

We repainted the exterior and peeled away the yellow tape still clinging to the trim from when the tiny house crossed the ocean. Sometimes we'd stop mid-task to admire the saguaro nearby, its crown in full bloom — a new flower each day. Lori sorted the plastic storage bins for travel while I rearranged the small shed on the south side, securing it with a key-lock box for whomever might need to work on the structure while we were gone. Above us, Neko observed it all from his favorite perch on the loft ladder, the quiet foreman of our leaving.

One morning, I drove to Starbucks to get out of the way while Lori finished the touch-ups. The barista asked what I had planned for the day. I said, "We're getting ready to leave." She smiled politely, not realizing that sentence carried a month of emotion.

There's a strange rhythm to endings. You plan, you prepare, and then at some point, the planning becomes the point.

I caught myself opening the same "to-do" note three times one morning, not because I'd forgotten what was on it, but because it gave me the illusion of control. I could hold the list and feel productive. I could tell myself we were "getting things ready."

But the truth is, no one's ever ready. Not for endings, not for transitions, not for the quiet that follows both.

It reminds me of how we do meetings back home—every week, the same agenda, the same reports, the same call for updates. We tell ourselves the repetition builds consistency, but what it really builds is habit. Familiarity. The comfort of movement without much motion.

Persistence, though, is something else. It's not efficiency; it's endurance. It's the willingness to show up, even when the plan doesn't help anymore.

I'm good under pressure because the deadlines remove the illusion of choice. I stop tinkering and start finishing. But these past few days, there's no hard deadline—just a slow fade of tasks and time. It's teaching me a different kind of persistence: staying steady when the finish line isn't visible.

Many evenings, I walk the same short loop behind the house.

Past the wash. Past the saguaros. Past the spot where we watched the sunset our first week here, back when everything still felt wide open. The desert looks the same, but it feels different—less like arrival, more like memory.

That's the real lesson of this place. You don't conquer a desert; you coexist with it. It doesn't reward completion. It rewards attention.

On our last night, we stood in the kitchen surrounded by packed boxes. As had become our habit since moving here, I jigsawed the boxes into the back of the Maverick, pulled the bed cover closed, and loaded the bikes onto the rear hitch carrier. We were ready for the trip back. I walked inside to give the thumbs-up that all was done and washed my hands.

I turned off the last light, opened the door, and looked out toward Panther Peak. The sky was the same pale blue it had been every morning since January. A few doves called from the fence line. Nothing dramatic, no swelling music, no clear line between staying and leaving.

Just a pause long enough to breathe in and say, we were here.

...

Your Turn:

Where are you preparing so much you've stopped being present?

How would it change your leaving—or your staying—if you walked the space one more time, just to notice?

The Persistence of Steps

A May hike with Jan, a few false peaks, and the rhythm that carried us home.

Jan (pronouced "Yawn") came to visit two weekends before we were set to leave.. It felt right that he'd see the desert with us before we packed up, before the heat came fully. He'd been asking since winter—"Mind if I come out and see your place?"— and we'd promised him hikes, sunsets, maybe a porch beverage. By the time he arrived that May morning, the saguaros were blooming, the lizards fast, and the air already warm by nine.

We set out for Wasson Peak, the tallest rise in the Tucson Mountain Range, carrying more water than pride. The trailhead at Esperanza cuts across a sandy wash before tilting abruptly upward—rocks loose, switchbacks mean, sun, direct. It's not a hike for small talk, though Jan tried, between breaths, to marvel at the view. He's a pastor by temperament, a question-asker by habit, so he noticed what most miss—the sound of bees in the brittlebush, the smell of creosote after another hiker's water bottle spilled. He captured much of it with his camera phone.

Seven minutes in, he met his first cholla.

That's the desert's version of baptism.

A soft "oh," a quick lift of his arm, and there it was—spines embedded, stubborn as memory. Out came the yellow comb we carry just for such moments. One pop, one laugh, one story already earned.

The climb that followed was slower. Every ridge promised the top, and every ridge lied. We'd crest what looked like the summit only to see another rise ahead, higher, hungrier. Jan would glance at me—"This it?"—and I'd grin. "Just another twenty minutes." It became our refrain, the shared joke that masked fatigue and named hope.

Somewhere along those false peaks, we stopped guessing.

We just walked.

That's the quiet gift of persistence. You trade prediction for presence.

When we finally reached the real top, the desert spread out below like a folded map: the red streak of the Hughes Trail, the gray wash curling through Picture Rocks, Tucson a faint shimmer to the east. We signed the small summit register, ate granola bars, shared trail mix, and let the silence do the talking. Wind tugged at our shirts. The sun pressed steady on our backs. For a few minutes, everything felt in proportion—our effort, our insignificance, our joy.

The descent was where the learning came.. Going down requires a different kind of strength—knees soft, mind alert. The same rocks that looked harmless now seemed treacherous. We saw more color, more texture, more of what we'd missed when we were so intent on climbing. I realized then that the desert rewards those who look twice.

Maybe life does too.

By the time we reached the truck, our water was gone and our hats spotted with salt. The air smelled of dust and mesquite. Jan leaned against the door and said, "That last peak—what a trick." We laughed, because it wasn't really a trick. It was a teaching: that what feels like the end rarely is, and that persistence isn't about reaching the top—it's about learning to rest, then rise again.

That evening, we drove over to the MSA Annex—clean, tired, grateful. Over dinner we replayed the day in gestures and half-sentences. The false peaks. The view. The quiet descent.

The next day, Sunday, we took another hike—shorter, gentler, easier to talk through life and scenery and such. Later, before his flight out of Mesa, Jan and I grabbed coffee and talked about the weekend—and what we hoped to do next with the land. (We'd spent that late morning walking the property, marking spots where another structure could go.) And then, he was off on I-10 to make the direct flight to South Bend, IN.

That afternoon, Lori and I started back on the to-do list on the trip back to Indiana.

Later, sitting on the deck and admiring our view of Wasson Peak, I kept thinking about that hike—how every ending looks like arrival until you turn around and see how far there still is to go.

The mountains always wait. The trail remains.

Step. Breath. Step.

. . .

Your Turn:

When have you thought you'd arrived—and then realized there was more climb left?

Describe one false peak—literal or metaphorical.

What changed once you kept walking?

"The Road Not Yet Paved"

On Twin Peaks Road and other long projects that teach us how to wait well.

The road between Casa Saguaro and Starbucks was never finished. Twin Peaks Road—connecting Sandario to Silverbell through a new stretch of desert housing and a narrow pass between hills—was being expanded.

Every week, the cones shifted just enough to make you wonder if progress was being made or if they were simply rehearsing the idea of progress. By now, I'd learned to slow down without complaint—windows up, not tailgating the car in front of me, playlist on low, the desert wind kicking up the caution flags.

If I left before six, I'd catch the crew gathering along the new lanes. They'd form a loose circle in the pink light, boots dusted from yesterday, hard hats tucked under their arms. The foreman would speak—briefly, clearly—and then everyone peeled off to their stations.

No ceremony. No lengthy kickoff meeting.

Just a few words, a nod, and work.

There was something quietly holy about that circle.

Focus without spectacle. Commitment without applause.

…

And I would see that same thing again, a month or so later, hundreds of miles away.

I was on I-57, driving one of two twenty-six-foot trucks, helping Tim and Jennifer move from South Carolina to Ames,

Iowa. The morning was long and flat, the kind that erases your sense of speed until a flash of orange barrels brings you back to yourself.

Traffic slowed to a crawl. Trucks were told to stay left. Everyone else merged right. We idled together through the heat shimmer, inch by inch toward the work zone.

When I finally reached the heart of it, I saw a foreman unfold a piece of paper handed to him by a man in khakis—a civil engineer, maybe. They were working on the water system— pipes stacked along the shoulder, heavy equipment idling nearby. The foreman studied the plans, nodded once, and waved the backhoe forward. Dust rose, sunlight caught on rebar, and for a few seconds, the whole scene looked choreographed.

It struck me then: everything solid takes time.

Whether it's a road, a deck, or a life, the work always outlasts the schedule.

. . .

I've built two decks, each time imagining it would take a weekend.

Felt like weeks.

Boards weren't level, screws stripped, plans stretched.

But the slowness changed something in me.

There's a stage in every project when progress flattens. You're still showing up, but the payoff hides. It's the plateau—the stretch where motivation dries up and patience starts doing the heavy lifting.

Someone once told me it takes fifteen to eighteen weeks to learn a new skill—to go from curiosity to competence. I've come to believe that's true of almost everything worth keeping. The real work isn't speed; it's return.

. . .

Building anything—habits, furniture, writing—depends on repetition and recalibration. You do the day's work, assess what's done, and begin again tomorrow.

That's what I admired about the Twin Peaks crew. They

started each morning with that small, intentional circle. "Here's the focus. Let's go." And then they went—no lingering, no over-explaining. The day's practice began before the sun had fully risen.

Maybe that's what persistence looks like: a series of small, faithful beginnings.

...

By the time I left Starbucks later in the day, the cones had shifted again, the line of progress moved a few feet forward.

No one watching would call it finished.

But something had changed.

And maybe that's enough.

Because the truth is, none of us are building at the speed we imagined.

But if we keep showing up—checking the plans, laying the next board, grading the next inch—we're already becoming builders of our own long roads.

...

Your Turn:

What small work deserves your repetition?
What could you build inch by inch if you kept showing up?

Persist Wrap (Marathon / Circles of Change)

This is the long work.

You've tracked a change, noticed a pattern, or maybe started a small loop.

Maybe now you see what lasts.

Maybe you notice what brings you back.

What kept you going?

What fell apart and got rebuilt?

What's worth doing again — tomorrow?

The circle always begins again.

It doesn't matter where.

Just return.

Practice Apps — Where Reflection Meets Action

The reflections in *Start Anywhere* invite new ways of seeing; these three apps invite new ways of doing.

They were born from the same questions that shape the book:

How do we begin? How do we follow through? How do we keep going when change feels slow?

Each app offers a different entry point — a space to write, to act, to notice — but all three share one intention:

to help you turn reflection into motion, and motion back into meaning.

Practice Apps — Begin, Act, Reflect

These three small tools were created alongside *Start Anywhere* as living extensions of its practice. Each one began as an experiment — something I needed to stay grounded, focused, and intentional in my own life. Together, they form a rhythm:
Engage through The Vestibule
Reduce through Turn
Persist through Circles of Change
They are not meant as productivity tools, but as invitations to return — to yourself, your work, and your relationships.

Access the Companion Apps

Access the apps at:
apps.vergilscoffeetable.com
Username: vctreader
Password: start2026

For updates and future releases:
Visit vergilscoffeetable.com
or subscribe to the newsletter at
vergilscoffeetable.substack.com

123

The Vestibule — A Place for Quiet Focus and Uninterrupted Writing

(Engage — Where You Begin)

Every good beginning needs a threshold. The Vestibule is that space — a quiet room between the noise of the day and the work that waits to be written. It exists to help you pause, focus, and begin from nothing.

I built it because I know myself: most of the time, I just need to begin. There are days when I can't find the motivation or willpower to start, when I keep waiting for inspiration that never comes. I used to rely on an old app called Write or Die — a quirky little program that turned writing into a game, flashing warnings if I hesitated too long. When it disappeared, I realized how much I'd depended on that nudge to stop overthinking and simply write.

So I made my own version. The Vestibule began as a rough Python script during my move to the desert — a quiet companion that let me set a timer, name a session, and write without distraction. Over time, it became a small daily ritual: fifteen minutes of honest drafting, no pasting, no editing, no excuses. Whether I'm warming up for a blog post or just clearing mental clutter, this is where I start.

If fifteen minutes feels like too much at first, start with five. Then ten. Then fifteen. Habits build like doors — one threshold at a time.

When you're ready, open The Vestibule, set a timer, and begin writing. Don't worry about making sense. Just keep your pen or cursor moving. What matters is that you've entered.

Micro-Prompt:
Set a timer for 5–15 minutes and begin with this line:
"Today, I'm standing at the doorway of..."
...

Turn — A Record of Follow-Through

(Reduce — Where Intention Becomes Movement)

Every promise begins with a turn — a small pivot from intention to action. Turn grew out of a season when I was full of plans but light on follow-through. I had lists on my iPad, reminders in half a dozen places, and yet I wasn't doing the things I said I would — especially the things I'd promised Lori.

So I built something simple. At first it was a rough Python app called I Said I Would, a small way to track what I'd promised, for whom, and by when. I figured that if I could make the tool both quiet and slightly amusing, I might actually use it. Later, on a trip to Wisconsin, I rebuilt it as a web app so I could carry it with me. I renamed it Turn — a nod to the moment when intention meets motion, and to the "turn-taking" that keeps relationships healthy.

Unlike most productivity tools, Turn isn't about managing everything. It's about honoring one thing. You choose a single promise — what you'll do, who it's for, when you'll return to it — and you follow it through. When you've done it, you don't mark it done; you mark it turned. That small shift in language reminds you that growth happens not through hustle but through motion — a quiet rotation toward what matters most. And every so often, Turn invites you to pause and look back — to notice patterns in your promises, moments of follow-through, or subtle turns that reveal where your energy and care have been leading you. Reflection is part of the motion.

Micro-Prompt:

Write one promise you want to keep this week.

Name who or what it's for, and take the first small turn toward it today.

...

Circles of Change — A Guided Journey from Vergil's Coffee Table

(Persist — Where Reflection Becomes Renewal)

Change rarely happens in straight lines. It loops, doubles back, and asks for patience. Circles of Change began as a way to see those slow movements — not as resolutions to chase, but as spirals to notice.

The idea came to me on a long run along the Pumpkinvine Trail in Middlebury, when I was thinking about what it really takes to sustain change. I'd been reading Michael Bungay Stanier's *The Coaching Habit* and was drawn to his simple framework for building habits: When this happens... instead of... I will. I loved the practicality of it, but I wanted something that also honored reflection — a way to not just do differently but to see differently.

At the same time, I kept thinking of the teaching book series *Not This, But This* — its invitation to move from the familiar, to understand why, and to choose better. I combined those two frameworks into what became Circles of Change: a tool to name a shift, explore what drives it, and trace how it unfolds over time.

The first versions were clunky. After the rush of creating The Vestibule and Turn, building Circles felt slow and tedious. But when I moved it to the web and began visualizing the process as actual circles — expanding rings of reflection stored privately on the user's device — it finally clicked. Turn captures the small daily actions; Circles holds the longer rhythm, the behaviors that evolve slowly, almost invisibly. I don't call them habits or resolutions. They're simply circles — reminders that change keeps coming back until we're ready to see it.

Micro-Prompt:
Name one small shift you've noticed lately — in habit, thought, or rhythm.
Write a few lines about what began that change and what's keeping it alive.

...

The Practice of Returning

Each of these tools began as a small experiment — a way to stay honest about where attention, effort, and change actually begin. The Vestibule helps you enter. Turn helps you follow through. Circles of Change helps you look back and see the shape of what's been forming. Together, they offer a rhythm more than a system: begin, act, reflect, repeat.

I created these apps because I needed them. I wanted to become more intentional — not just in my work, but in my relationships with the people around me: with Lori, Evan, and Colin; with colleagues and friends; with the teachers I coach and the students they serve. Even the small, chance conversations — the ones that happen at Goshen Brewing Company or along a trail in Tucson — remind me that most of what matters depends on presence and follow-through. These apps became a quiet accountability: not to productivity, but to connection.

For someone else, a simple notebook might do the same thing. But for me, having these three small icons on my phone keeps that intention visible. They remind me that technology doesn't have to fracture my attention — it can focus it. The Vestibule opens a blank space for reflection. Turn helps me name and keep a promise. Circles of Change invites me to notice what's shifting over time. Each one asks for something small: a few words, a few minutes, a return.

That act of noticing — even without judging or fixing — is where change begins. Over time, these moments of entry, follow-through, and reflection begin to form their own pattern, a kind of circle that widens quietly. The more I return to the practice, the more I see that life doesn't move in straight lines.

It loops back, deepens, and reminds us that the smallest beginnings can still carry us forward.

And so we return again — ready to begin anywhere.

Afterword — Create Your Own Metaphor

This isn't a book that ends; it's one that opens again.

You've walked alongside three metaphors:

Engage, through the Torii gates — places of entry, attention, and beginning.

Reduce, through the tiny house — spaces shaped by choice and care.

Persist, through the marathon — a practice of returning, step by step.

Each of these began as my own attempts to notice a rhythm I wanted to live by.

They were never meant to be permanent fixtures—only doorways.

You may find that your life speaks another language.

Maybe your threshold isn't a gate but a trailhead.

Maybe your version of the tiny house is a studio, a classroom, or a crowded kitchen table.

Maybe your marathon shows up in recovery, parenting, caregiving, or creation.

However it appears, the invitation is familiar:

to notice where you are,

to loosen what no longer needs to be carried,

to stay with what matters long enough to see what it becomes.

What metaphors are already showing up in your life?

What do they seem to ask of you?

You might take a moment to name one—quietly, or in writing.

You don't need to explain it to anyone else.

You can simply live alongside it and see what it begins to teach.

That's the point of this whole circle:

not to follow my metaphors,

but to discover your own.

These three—the Gates, the House, the Run—are just ways to begin.

Your life will offer others.

The circle keeps turning.

So whenever you're ready,

return.

If You'd Like to Sit With This a Little Longer

What image or space keeps returning in your life lately?
What might it be trying to teach you?
How will you listen to it this week?

Coffee Notes

Some clarifications, references, and things you might have wondered about:

Why "Vergil" and not "Virgil"?
The version of Dante's *Inferno* I first read spelled it with an "e," and it stuck. I've used that spelling ever since—on Twitter, in early drafts, and now here. Also, it looks better typographically.

Circle of Concern vs. Circle of Influence
That framing comes from *The 7 Habits of Highly Effective People* by Stephen Covey. I first encountered it as a young teacher in a PD session, and Habit #5 ("Seek First to Understand, then to be Understood") still shapes how I think about how I understand the role of empathy and my relationships.

Starbucks (yes, I noticed too)
An early reader kindly pointed out I mention Starbucks a lot (15 times). Fair. I do much of my best thinking in coffee shops. The two I frequent—one in Goshen, Indiana, the other in Marana, Arizona—are welcoming, predictable, and staffed by managers who embody quiet leadership. Marissa, Raina: thank you for running the kind of place where people get real work done.

Round Table Pizza
There's a discrepancy of which pizza restaurant that Russ and I almost got kicked out of (Russ mentioned this in the comment section of the original blog post). I remember it as the place off Farmers Lane and Bennett Valley Road. I suppose that's how memory works.

Section Pictures
Since I didn't caption the pictures, here's the information of each: Engage: Torri Gates: Lori and Me selfie: 29 June 2024; Reduce: Tiny House at Casa Saugaro at Night: 29 April 2025; Persist: Maple City Indoor Marathon (204 laps), Goshen College, Goshen, IN: 05 March 2017.

"Do you want to know what my secret is? I don't mind what happens"
The quote is referenced in MBS' *Do Something that Matters Journal* (125) and is attributed to Jiddu Krishnamurti and I verified it via ChatGPT <g>.

Spelling and sound
Yes, that's "Jan" (rhyming with yawn). And no, my California-born vowel blending isn't lost on my speech-therapist wife.

Middlebury's "Estate at Mineral Springs" and the Arizona tiny house "Casa Saguaro"
Two places, two kinds of building projects. Naming them helps me see them not just as locations, but as part of our ongoing design — of home, of life, of attention.

Enneagram 7
The Enneagram is a nine-type framework for understanding patterns of motivation and attention. Over time, it has given Lori and me a shared vocabulary—one that helps us speak more gently about our differences, recognize our similarities, and return to one another with greater awareness. The "7" is sometimes referred as the "Enthusiast."

A note on the apps
If the digital tools feel like too much right now—skip them. You can always return later. I built each app to meet a personal need: to begin again, to commit gently, or to reflect during a transition. They're companions, not requirements.

About the Author

Chris Judson, author of *Start Anywhere*, writes and reflects from the Arizona desert and northern Indiana. (2 Dec 2025)

About the Author

Chris Judson is a writer, educator, and desert dweller who splits his time between Northern Indiana and the Arizona desert. He and his wife, Lori, have been married for over thirty-five years and share life with two adult sons, Evan and Colin, who both make music, and a not-so-calm cat named Neko.

Start Anywhere is Chris's first book. He is the founder of *Vergil's Coffee Table*, a reflective practice studio at the intersection of metaphor, writing, and change. With decades of experience teaching, running marathons, and drinking good coffee, Chris writes with the hope that if you and he ever find yourselves sharing a beverage, you'll already feel like old friends.

Colophon

This book was written over the course of 2025 — most often on a 13-inch MacBook Air (M3), wrapped in a hard shell case featuring *The Great Wave off Kanagawa* by Katsushika Hokusai.

Drafts began in The Vestibule — a custom writing app built to invite presence — or as voice memos recorded on an iPhone while walking, driving, or returning home.

Much of the writing took place at favorite tables in two coffee shops — in Twin Peaks (Tucson), Arizona, and Goshen, Indiana — where a second cup and a quiet corner helped the words arrive.

The manuscript was organized and edited in Ulysses, then exported using the Paperback style by David Hewson.

The body text is set in Cochin, a serif typeface inspired by 18th-century French copperplate engravings.

Headings are set in Futura, a modern, contrasting geometric sans serif font.

The creative process was grounded in the *Do Something That Matters* journal by Michael Bungay Stanier.

This book was printed via print-on-demand through KDP and IngramSpark.

It was made slowly, on purpose.

Vergil's Coffee Table

This book is part of a growing collection of reflections, questions, and creative tools offered under the name Vergil's Coffee Table — a small imprint and creative space built to honor the slow work of becoming.

At its heart, Vergil's Coffee Table is about thresholds, returnings, and circles of change — moments when we pause long enough to notice where we are, and wonder where we might be going.

Thank you for joining me here.

Peace,
Chris
vergilscoffeetable.com